FISH & DIVE FLORIDA

and The Keys

A Candid Destination Guide

by

M.Timothy O'Keefe and Larry Larsen

Book 3 in the Outdoor Travel Series
by Larsen's Outdoor Publishing

Please note that all factual information such as names, addresses, and telephone numbers listed in this book are subject to change.

ISBN 0-936513-26-8

Library of Congress 92-090226

Published by:

LARSEN'S OUTDOOR PUBLISHING
2640 Elizabeth Place
Lakeland, FL 33813

Senior Editor: Lilliam Morse Larsen

PRINTED IN THE UNITED STATES OF AMERICA

2 3 4 5 6 7 8 9 10

NATIONAL AWARDS

Fish & Dive The Caribbean, Vol. 1 by Larry Larsen and M. Timothy O'Keefe was one of the three top finalists in the 1991 Best Book Content Category competition of the National Association of Independent Publishers (NAIP).

Fish & Dive The Caribbean, Vol. 1 was one of over 500 books submitted by U.S. publishers, including Simon & Schuster and Turner Publishing, Inc. (CNN).

Said the NAIP judges of *Fish & Dive The Caribbean, Vol.1,* "An excellent source book with invaluable instructions for fishing or diving. Written by two nationally-known experts who, indeed, know what vacationing can be!"

Now, these same authors have brought their vast expertise to their own back yard in their newest book *Fish & Dive Florida And The Keys.*

PREFACE

Like a close friend relating his latest adventures, authors M. Timothy O'Keefe and Larry Larsen provide a unique personal insight to the experience of diving and fishing the country's Sunshine state.

As free lance writers and photographers, both Timothy and Larry have traveled the state over the past 20 years to fulfill numerous assignments. Much of the information gleaned from these trips cannot be incorporated into their magazine articles due to lack of space. In *Fish & Dive Florida & The Keys*, the authors have revisited many of the best (and worst) fishing and diving experiences.

It is very improbable that divers and anglers of all skill levels would not learn something from this book. Written with a personal perspective, there is no better way to truly discover all the opportunities for fishing and diving, where to go, when and how to enjoy the trip.

DEDICATION

We would like to dedicate this work to Karl Wickstrom, publisher, and the late Bill Hallstrom, first executive editor, of "Florida Sportsman" Magazine. Making us editors-at-large for the publication in the early 1970s gave us the freedom and the motivation to explore and photograph all over Florida. Thanks, guys; it's been an exciting and rewarding life. It wouldn't have been nearly as much fun without you.

M. Timothy O'Keefe
and Larry Larsen

CONTENTS

ABOUT THE AUTHORS

M. Timothy O'Keefe

M. Timothy O'Keefe has been a diver and fisherman for more than 30 years. His articles and photos have appeared in many publications, including National Geographic Society books, Time Life Books, *Travel & Leisure, Newsweek, Rodale's Scuba Diving, Skin Diver, SCUBA Times, Caribbean Travel & Life, Saltwater Sportsman, Power & Motoryacht* and many others. He was editor of *The International Divers Guide* and *Diver's World*. Tim holds a Ph D. from the University of North Carolina at Chapel Hill and is a professor in the School of Communication at the University of Central Florida in Orlando, where he established the journalism program. He is a member of the Outdoor Writers Association of America (OWAA) and the Society of American Travel Writers (SATW). His fishing and diving articles and photos have received numerous awards over the years.

Larry Larsen

An angler for 40 years and certified diver for more than 20 years, Larry Larsen has traveled Florida extensively in search of fishing and diving opportunities. His articles and photos have appeared in numerous regional and national outdoor/travel magazines. Larry is Florida Editor for *Outdoor Life*, and contributor to *Florida Sportsman, Saltwater Sportsman, Marlin, Sport Fishing, Southern Saltwater, Caribbean Travel & Life* and many other magazines. He is a member of the Outdoor Writers Association of America (OWAA), the Florida Outdoor Writers Association (FOWA) and the National Association of Independent Publishers (NAIP) and has been honored with many awards for his writing, publishing and photography. Larry holds a Master's from Colorado State University. He has authored 14 books on fishing and as President of Larsen's Outdoor Publishing, has published several titles on the outdoors.

INTRODUCTION

More than 8,000 miles of relatively unpolluted coastline, Gulf Stream-swept clear waters, natural and artificial reefs, and a network of freshwater springs make Florida a land of opportunity for anglers and divers alike. Warm waters from the Gulf Stream bath the mid-Atlantic south to the Keys and influence the Gulf on the west coast north to Tampa Bay.

The resulting sub-tropical environment impacts waters off the barrier island system along the Atlantic, the mangrove islands on the lower west coast, and the salt-marsh estuaries of the upper Gulf coast. The abundance and variety of marine life in Florida's coastal waters is unsurpassed in this country. It deserves attention and respect, meaning that we should all try to enjoy it and conserve it.

The state's saltwater fishing opportunities are seasonal in many cases, and the table in each fishing chapter reveals the most common species that are caught during each season of the year. Each handy table should be used as a guide to pre-plan a trip after the most common species available then. Information in the text will often elaborate on the opportunities in each region.

As the water temperature warms, sailfish move north in the spring along the Loop Current in the Gulf of Mexico. On the Atlantic side, they move north with the Gulf Stream. In the late fall, decreasing water temperature and a southerly migration of baitfish motivate the sails to retrace their travels back south along both coasts.

Spanish and king mackerel move northward each spring along both coasts from their winter ocean home off the lower one-third of

Florida's peninsula. Similarly, tarpon move north and south at the dictates of the seasonal weather and spawning urges, and the popular three-some of redfish, snook and trout move from shallow flats to deeper waters with colder water temperatures.

Pods of cobia migrate north and west along panhandle coasts from Steinhatchee to Pensacola each March. By April, they inhabit the markers and artificial reefs over the entire area. On the Atlantic side, cobia are abundant in northeast coast in the summer months. During the fall and winter, they take up residence along the central Gulf coast and lower east coast.

The Diving

Floridians have known all along they have the best diving in the Northern Hemisphere. Visitors acknowledge it, too, and more than two million of them from all over the world visit the Florida Keys annually, making it the most dived location on earth.

Floridians have always suspected --but it's always nice to have it confirmed by an outsider--that the Sunshine State also has the nation's best beaches. We were right, too.

According to a 1991 study by Stephen Leatherman, Director of the University of Maryland's Laboratory for Coastal Research, Florida has 7 of America's 10 finest beaches and 15 of the top 20.

The most highly ranked beaches are not in South Florida as you might expect, but in the most northerly region, The Panhandle. Although these beach rankings deal with the coastline, what you'll find underwater will be just as surprising as you explore Florida's vast marine park. Not only are Panhandle beaches outstanding, but visibility there can also be incredibly good, equaling or surpassing any other part of the state.

Each underwater section of Florida is vastly different from the other. It's been said Florida is really three separate states-- The Panhandle, Central Florida and South Florida--combined into one. The underwater regions contain such a magnificent scope of diversity to reflect a whole different universe.

But it is a potentially hostile universe, more receptive to visitors at certain times than others. Florida's best diving is from April/May to October. That is the period of calmest and clearest water and, in truth, the only time to plan an extended dive vacation unless you have time and money to burn. If you want a sure thing, wait until summer. Even then, diving may be limited primarily to the morning because of the frequent afternoon thundershowers which send everyone scampering for shore. If you always schedule your two tanks for the morning, afternoons become more of an option: for another dive or to sight-see on land, always worth doing.

Remember, travel posters and travel ads depict the ideal image of Florida, not reality. Even the fabled Keys are virtually undiveable whenever a winter cold front passes through. Waves of 5-6 feet or more may keep boats at the dock for days at a time unless you can round up enough Rambo divers to go out whatever the conditions, hellish and high water. Storms also stir up the bottom and reduce visibility for days.

Don't expect to come to Florida and find good ocean diving every time of the year. And bring a full wet suit for fall, winter and early spring. The water may be warm enough for bathers who dash in and out, but not for divers who stay submerged for an hour at a time. Even bold Canadians who attempt to dive the Keys in winter without wet suits return to the boat with their teeth sounding like castanets.

Florida's best salt water diving is on the Atlantic side, from the Palm Beaches to Key West and the Dry Tortugas. As explained in a later chapter, this is the region with the living coral reef, which is the underpinning of Florida's unique marine ecosystem.

In winter, the best diving is actually in fresh water, in the massive spring system found throughout the Panhandle and Central Florida. Divers come from as far away as Texas and Tennessee for long weekend trips in fresh water then, knowing the springs are the place to find consistently clear water and no adverse wind conditions. However, many springs are affected by rain runoff and may cloud up for a few days following a deluge. In the springtime, many fresh water springs along the Santa Fe and Suwannee are affected by the rising, discolored river waters. While the caverns and tunnels may remain clear because of the repeated flushing action of the cold water currents, the spring basins may look like they need a good application of Tidy Bowl or some other cleansing preparation.

The moral: always check conditions ahead of your arrival. You definitely will find many good places in Florida to dive all year round if you are willing to accept the limitations imposed by the weather. Our travel promotion industry has given many visitors the impression that Florida is paradise year-round. Not quite, but I wouldn't be surprised if the imagineers at Orlando's Disney World aren't working on it.

Fishing Activity Capsule

Most of Florida's saltwater fish are caught all along the state's coastline, but fishing for a particular species may be better in one area than in another. The following are species most often encountered in Florida:

SOUTH FLORIDA

The Keys- Trout and redfish (Upper Keys), snapper, bonefish, permit, tarpon; grouper, amberjack, barracuda, sails and wahoo.

South Atlantic Coast - Sailfish, marlin, tuna, mako shark and dolphin in the Gulf Stream. Inshore - snook, tarpon, bluefish, trout and mackerel during runs.

South Gulf Coast- Tarpon, snook and redfish; pompano, mackerel during runs.

CENTRAL FLORIDA

West Gulf Coast - Tarpon, Snook, cobia, trout, kingfish, mackerel, grouper

East Atlantic Coast - Trout, redfish, drum, tripletail, jack crevalle, sailfish and snook.

NORTH FLORIDA

Northwest Gulf Coast - Trout, redfish, flounder, grouper, tarpon in summer; mangrove snapper in fall; offshore runs of cobia, kingfish, mackerel in spring.

Northeast Atlantic Coast - Redfish, bluefish, trout, drum, and tarpon.

1

THE KEYS TO BLUE WATER ANGLING

Larry's favorite winter action is off the Gold Coast and the Florida Keys

The best sailfishing in the Atlantic? Ask any knowledgeable offshore angler, and he will tell you it undoubtedly takes place along Florida's "Gold Coast" and upper Keys. The prime waters extend from West Palm Beach south past Key Largo, the first island in the Florida Keys. Year in and year out, this stretch of the Atlantic Ocean provides the most consistent sailfish action.

The Gulf Stream moves close to the land here, and a rapid drop in depth allows sails and other large sportfish to feed near the coast. Sailfishing peaks after each brush with cool weather during the winter.

"Around the third week in December, the sails begin showing up, and the season usually lasts through April," says Captain Pierre Pierce. "The best fishing seems to be just about six miles off Ocean Reef Club. On one half day trip, we caught seven sailfish!"

Much of the sailfish action takes place in water depths of 100 to 300 feet. Captains like Pierce prefer to begin their day's fishing for sails at the shallows of that range and then work toward the deeper waters. They'll usually employ small ballyhoo for bait and will either fish them live as they drift in such depths, or slow-troll dead ballyhoo behind a rubber skirt over the same waters.

Captain Pierce is a sailfish enthusiast who has spent over 20 years fishing the area from Ocean Reef Club on the north end of Key Largo to the Gulf Stream off Fort Lauderdale. The Miamian captained large sportfishing boats for Bertram yachts for several years and enjoys the sailfish action, particularly when multiple hookups occur. Pierce once had five sails strike his baits at one time, and his fishermen caught and released every one of them.

On my first trip to Ocean Reef, I covered their annual Reef Cup Invitational Sailfish Tournament for Outdoor Life magazine. I also had an opportunity to fish aboard a 41-foot Bertram with Captain Pierce. The setting for perhaps the premier sailfishing event in North America was the beautiful Ocean Reef Club, a 4,000 acre resort and development which includes one of the largest marinas in the southeast, boat storage, charter service, airport, dining and shopping areas. Best of all the destination has 2,000 acres set aside for a permanent wildlife preserve and is just a short boat ride from the area's best sailfishing.

The three day tournament was wrapping up when my wife, Lilliam, and I met Pierce and our mate for the day, Captain Brian Nemeth. Spinning tackle comprised the battle weapons that day, and the lines spooled on the light reels were 20 pound test. The medium heavy spinning rods were 7 1/2 feet long and sized to take the punishment of a sail.

Ballyhoo is considered the best bait for the sailfish off the entire Gold Coast region, and both Pierce and Nemeth prefer live bait when available. That day it was. We spent an hour chumming the proper bait over a reef on the way to our fishing grounds. We caught several of the ballyhoo on a small hook and pieces of shrimp and squid before Nemeth used a cast net to secure another two dozen on his first attempt. The bait survived fine in the aerated live well.

While several of the tournament boats were fishing by drifting live bait with kites, Captain Pierce preferred drifting the four ballyhoo off outriggers in search of the sail. It was 10:30 a.m. and we didn't have to wait long for action.

The rigger clip sprang with the tension of a fish. I grabbed the rod, and the battle was on. The captain, preferring not to "back-down" on the sail (reverse the engine and aid the angler in getting the fish to the boat quicker), let me fight it to the boat. The small

Charter boats are available at the beautiful Ocean Reef Marina for billfishing, bonefishing, tarpon and bottom fishing.

sail put up a respectable battle against the 20-pound tackle, but was soon at the transom, where Nemeth released it by cutting the leader near the embedded hook.

Not a bad start, we all thought. Yet, that was the only sail action we had, and after lunch, we changed tactics. Nemeth and Pierce knew of king mackerel schools roving the area, so we tried to raise one of them. After about 15 minutes of trolling, Lilliam caught a respectable mackerel. Two or three other fish were taken before we returned to the 175-slip Ocean Reef Marina, ahead of the tournament boats.

Of the 39 boats over 26 feet in length registered for the Reef Cup, eight caught a sailfish that day. We considered ourselves very lucky. Over the three days, the tournament fleet caught 36 sails, and the top boat, captained by Joey Yerkes, was aptly named "Happy Hooker." Michael Wetterman caught and released four of the five sailfish brought to the stern of the "Happy Hooker" for top individual honors. All five of the fish were taken on days two and three.

Charter boats are available at the beautiful Ocean Reef Marina. For those who want a little variety, there are also bonefishing, tarpon fishing and bottom fishing charters. Only minutes away from the marina is John Pennekamp Coral Reef State Park. Scuba diving, snorkeling and glass-bottom boating to the watery wonderland is also available year around. For more information, write to Ocean Reef Club and Resort, Key Largo, Florida 33037 or phone (800) 741-REEF or (305) 367-2611.

Billfish Destinations

From West Palm Beach to the Alligator Reef off Islamorada, sailfish action increases with each mild cold front. It can be found most frequently using live bait. Popular methods include slow-trolling baitfish from outriggers, flat lines or kites. A good live well to contain the bait is paramount to the success of live-baiting.

● Blue marlin become active in the Gulfstream a little further offshore when the weather warms up and the sailfish action slows. Some top areas include the east and west humps, 25 miles southeast of the Sombrero light. Off Fort Lauderdale, marlin to 300 pounds are caught regularly during August and September by captains using downriggers and appropriate lures and bait.

High-speed trolling of artificials can also keep heat effects to a minimum and action maximum under a mid-day summer sun. More marlin are being caught at speeds of up to 15 knots in relatively calm seas during the hot months than other times.

● Many Gold Coast sportfishermen follow their "radio signals" to the hotspots that are frequently broadcast. Billfish move at a fairly consistent depth, from 80 to 350 feet and best times are during the morning or late afternoon hours. Marlin are usually taken at deeper depths.

There are plenty of great marinas along the Gold Coast that offer charter fishing opportunities. The Bahia Mar Resort & Yachting Center in Fort Lauderdale has a "Fishing Fleet" of 14 charter boats. The famous marina offers 350 slips off its 40-acre island retreat. Blue marlin off the Gold Coast average 250 to 300 pounds, but occasionally a 500 pounder is captured.

Dolphin Mania

Dolphin are the eager quarry for South Florida anglers in the summer. It's the prime time of the season with stable weather patterns, relatively calm seas and a build-up of weedlines in the Gulf Stream farther offshore. More running time may be involved, but the action is well worth it. Most dolphin are caught along the grassy "feedlines," rips, floating debris and water color changes. Such places should be the habitat focus of productive anglers.

Schools of dolphin often congregate under sargassum weedlines in search of both food and protection from predators. The grass lines are easy to see and the dolphin under them very willing to be

14

a major part of the action for the day. The early morning finds them particularly cooperative and the seas less crowded. The Atlantic waters off the South Florida coasts can get very busy with dolphin addicts around mid-day.

The close in weedlines are usually less dense than those to be found further offshore, and the successful anglers won't waste much time on them if they don't quickly produce. They keep moving looking for large patches of floating weeds and debris. Big floating objects such as boards or logs in the blue water several miles offshore are a magnet to big bull and cow dolphin.

They'll hit almost anything in the way of a lure or natural bait presented near their hangout. Some anglers troll the grass patches and move from one to another at full speed until they locate a school of dolphin. Others cast to each potential gathering ground for the first fish. Having casting tackle, a light spinning rod or fly rod pre-rigged for the action to follow is a wise move.

Once a fish strikes and the boat stops, the angler should "play it" until a second one from the school is hooked. It can then be landed and the second one left in the water until another is hooked. The school will continue to hang around a fighting fish that is perceived as feeding.

Often, it's possible to catch eight or ten fish averaging 15 pounds from the same school. Those 30 pounds and up are less common but available, particularly in deeper waters. On one trip to Islamorada, several friends and I were able to average about 30 dolphin each in one day. Most were small fish, and all but a few were released alive.

A yellow or white jig or fresh cut bait will attract dolphin off the Gold Coast. Chum in the form of small pieces of the natural bait can be effectively used in limited quantities to keep area fish active. Ballyhoo and finger mullet are favorite baits to toss into a school. Add a plastic skirt for maximum action on the giant specimens.

Unlike most fish, the male dolphin (bulls) grow larger than the females. They'll grow to between 15 and 35 pounds in less than one year, according to marine biologists, and only live to about four years of age. To become robust in a short time, they feed on crabs, flying fish, squid and other forage fish around the weedlines.

Their feeding urge, though, makes them vulnerable to overharvesting. They are one of the best-tasting fish swimming the ocean and one of the fastest growing, but remember to release all dolphin not destined for the grill or oven. Use gloves and care in handling while removing the hook.

August may be the final month of great summer dolphin action. You may have to search longer for the schools and the size could run smaller, up to 10 pounds on the average, but they are there.

White marlin around 50 pounds, king mackerel averaging 8 pound, wahoo of 15 to 20 pounds, and amberjack around 15 pounds are frequent catches off the Gold Coast. King mackerel often hang out during winter months in an area called "No Man's Land." The area of grass, shell and rock bottom is located southeast of the Dry Tortugas in 60 to 120 feet of water.

Tarpon and Bottom Fish

Bottom fishing around the Keys is productive after hours in the hot months, but be prepared for the onslaught of mosquitoes and no-seeums that often accompany sunset activities near the mangroves. Chumming the outer reefs and bay channels will attract a better concentration of fish, making any discomfort worthwhile.

Cubera snapper weighing up to 100 pounds are also eager biters off Key Largo in depths around 100 feet. Blue crab, shrimp or crayfish fished just off the bottom with a short wire leader and heavy tackle are all that's needed to have some fun. The prime time occurs around the full moon in August. Summer time action is also exciting for yellowtail, mutton and mangrove snappers over reefs.

● Snapper fishing in Florida Bay and the Everglades National Park is often good. Live shrimp, mullet, pinfish or cut bait all take their share of the tasty fish. Night angling for spawning mangrove snapper is a June treat.

It's party boat time year-round in South Florida and the Keys, and the bottom fishing is generally good. Fishing for large amberjack off "Gold Coast" wrecks and the lower Keys flats also is usually excellent. Cobia can be caught off the piers and inlet jetties as well.

● Tarpon will be on the ocean-side flats, adjacent to the bridges and passes all up and down the Keys. Buchanan Bank located south of Islamorada, and Nine-Mile Bank are good areas. Live crabs and pinfish fished on 30 to 40-pound test below the Keys bridges are favored baits and most productive in the spring months.

Tarpon will be on the ocean-side flats, adjacent to the bridges and passes all up and down the Keys.

● Later, tarpon are usually found in the "backcountry," from the Gulf side of U.S. Highway 1 to Flamingo in the Everglades National Park. Sandy Key Basin is an excellent spot. They can be found on the outside flats too. Some of the tarpon are migratory and move northward in and out of the creeks and passes with the tides.

Tarpon average about 20 pounds, but fish up to 100 pounds are taken fairly regularly. Spotted Jewfish from 25 to 50 pounds are sometimes taken in the same spots as tarpon, although some monsters over 100 pounds have been taken along the Gold Coast.

● The Northeast Hole, along the outer reef in 120 feet of water, lies northeast of Fort Lauderdale and offers good bottom fishing. The scattered rock, coral growth and rugged relief is great for snapper and grouper during the winter months. Another good spot is the 75-foot deep depression called "Snapper Hole" located about six miles off Pompano Beach. King mackerel also show up there.

● Snapper and grouper are plentiful in the Keys, around the "R.W. Flats" located in 200 feet of water south of the Dry Tortugas.

17

Snapper and grouper action over the area of coral rock and three sunken submarines is tops in the spring. There is a productive rock cliff in 50 to 120 feet of water southeast of Key West.

● The "Conch Reefs," in 30 to 60 feet of water offshore between Marathon and Islamorada, produce mutton and mangrove snapper and yellowtail, especially in the summer months. "Coffin's Patch" is a 20 to 100-feet-deep area between Marathon and Islamorada with scattered shipwrecks and dense coral surrounded by sand and grass. King mackerel, barracuda and dolphin are plentiful there.

● In the surf off the Gold Coast, look for whiting, croker, bluefish, pompano and Spanish mackerel in the cooler months. African pompano, blackfin tuna, barracuda, wahoo and dolphin are also active then. Trout fishing around the bayside grass flats in the Upper Keys to Cape Sable and redfish in the backcountry of the Upper Keys and Florida Bay are active in December and January.

180 Million Dollar Lure

Somewhere in South Florida lives an offshore fisherman who left behind a lure that was worth millions. He was trolling his plug over 60 foot depths southwest of Key West when it hung up on an obstruction projecting some 25 feet off the bottom: the wooden hull of the remains of the 1622 "Atocha" treasure wreck.

Had the unsuspecting angler jumped overboard to free his snagged plug, he probably would have noticed the unique structure. Beside the encrusted hull was a huge pile of silver bars with just a fine layer of silt covering them. In the same area lay pure silver ingots and "pieces of eight," thousands of them.

The Atocha treasure was the largest find in recent history. Certainly, the plug had not been snagged long before Mel Fisher and crew came along to discover their fortune. The moral: offshore sportfishermen should carry scuba tanks and snorkel gear along just in case they get hung up in fairly shallow water. The angler that lost his lure to the Atocha hull either wasn't equipped to retrieve it or just didn't bother going after the plug. After all, the lure probably wasn't worth over eight to 15 dollars... he thought.

Salvagers of this Keys wreck found the plug and wonder to this day who lost it. They call it the $180 million lure and for good reason!

2

DIVING FLORIDA'S CARIBBEAN

Tips from Tim's personal experience

There's a lot to be said for staying in your own backyard instead of journeying out of the country for a dive vacation. Remaining state-side, you avoid the inconvenience of immigration and customs lines, language barriers, unfavorable currency exchanges and all the general hassles of foreign travel.

Of course, it doesn't make much sense to stay at home if the diving isn't as good, but that's hardly a problem in the Florida Keys, America's version of the Caribbean and home to the only living coral reef in the Continental U.S.

Many of the Keys' marine plants and animals are primarily of Caribbean origin rather than North American since the Gulf Stream and trade winds forming the Keys environment carried the fish, birds and seed pods from the south. Consequently, the Keys are the northernmost habitat for many subtropical species. At least 52 species of coral and 500 species of fish have been counted in the Keys.

Calling the Keys "America's Caribbean Islands" isn't just advertising puffery; it's also a matter of scientific fact. Driving into Key Largo, it's immediately apparent you're in one of the dive capitals of the world--more than 2 million divers annually visit the Keys. Even so, it still seems strange that dive shops are located on almost every corner.

19

Or to go into a supermarket and find one of the first signs displayed is "Divers' RX corner," with an assortment of abrasion creams, ear remedies and sinus decongestants. Or pick up the local phone book to find a cover montage of a colorful cartoon fish wearing a sombrero, a moray eel with sun glasses and an octopus laughing so hysterically that it sheds tears. Furthermore, the Yellow Pages even have 5-1/2 pages of dive shop advertising.

This, indeed, is the Florida Keys, the diver's version of Mecca that every underwater swimmer expects to visit at least once during this lifetime. In all, there are 822 islands in the Keys chain large enough to be recorded on government charts, scores more of tiny mangrove clumps too small to be included. Only about 30 are inhabited. They extend for 120 miles, bounded by the Atlantic on the east and the Gulf of Mexico on the west, to form the southernmost point in the continental U.S.

The Keys are actually emergent reminders of the foothills of a very old part of the Appalachian Mountains which extended up into the mid-Atlantic states. The two-mile thick skeleton of an ancient coral reef resting atop the foothills forms the limited land mass of the Upper Keys. In the southern sector, a naturally cemented limestone rock known as Miami oolite forms the surfacing.

As throughout much of Florida, the Keys are developing rapidly with new shopping malls, restaurants and resorts opening all the time. The Key Largo of Humphrey Bogart and Lauren Bacall never existed, not even in the 1940s film classic of the same name; the stars never actually visited the Keys and only a few exterior scenes were filmed here. As for Ernest Hemingway's rugged old fishing town of Key West, it's evolved into a major resort city with one of the country's highest percentages of gays per capita. Except for a few hold-out spots, the rip-roaring Keys of yesterday have been totally sanitized and modernized.

The Keys, located only 40 miles southwest of Miami, are divided into three distinct regions, all offering good diving. A $185 million highway improvement project has replaced 37 of the old narrow bridges linking the island chain with modern, "widetrack" spans, so the drive all the way from Key Largo south to Key West takes only about 3 hours.

Please
DO NOT STEAL
THE SHARK TEETH
THEY ARE PLASTIC
NOT REAL!

Full day shark trips are not as suicidal as they may look.

So it's quite easy to move down the island chain whenever and to wherever you're inclined, sampling a wide variety of reefs, wrecks, fishing, shopping, dining and nightlife. A week is time enough, two would be better.

Weather

Although the Keys are similar to the Caribbean in many ways, the winter weather pattern is definitely not the Caribbean's. The calmest and clearest waters usually are in summer, from May through September. The rest of the year the wind sometimes blows hard enough that the dive boats don't even venture out because of the probability of everyone getting seasick. These adverse conditions sometimes come as a shock to people who arrive in the middle of winter and except to find summer-like sunny, calm weather.

Anytime a front barrels down the Atlantic Coast, the Keys will feel it just like everywhere else. The water gets just as choppy as off

21

North Florida or Georgia. It may also get considerably cooler, too, though temperatures below the 50s are extremely rare.

Wintertime in the Keys is also full wet suit weather. The Keys may have the warmest saltwater diving of anywhere in the country, but the water temperatures drop into the 60s or 70s. That's colder water than most divers can withstand for any period of time, no matter how healthy a layer of body fat.

Frankly, I've been blown out of the Keys so many times during winter I avoid them then because of the drive time from my Central Florida home. If you're traveling a fair distance and want to ensure you experience the Keys at their finest, go during summer. That's also when room rates are lowest and overall there are fewer visitors clogging the roads and waterways.

Adventure Dives

OK, so you've seen the Keys lots of times before, and you want something new and exciting to draw you back. How about becoming the main ingredient for shark fin soup?

What is believed to be the only dive anywhere on the East Coast where divers chum up sharks and then jump into the water with them is being offered through Conch Republic Divers at Mile Marker 91.5 in Tavernier.

The full day shark trips are not as suicidal as they may sound. Once the sharks are enticed to the boat, divers view them from the safety of a steel cage specially designed for just these excursions. Although several California dive shops offer the same experience, Conch Republic is the only Keys operation (and apparently the whole Eastern seaboard) with such a similar procedure.

Divers enter the cage while it is still out of the water, thereby avoiding a suspenseful swim from boat to cage and back. Dual tanks with 6-foot regulator hoses are locked in racks inside the cage, so divers enter only with masks, fins, weight belt and any desired camera equipment. Only two divers, accompanied by a divemaster, are in the cage at any one time.

The cage typically hangs at about 10 feet, which allows a leisurely 45-minute session for three-persons. Other divers waiting for their turn chill out by reading, relaxing or sunbathing.

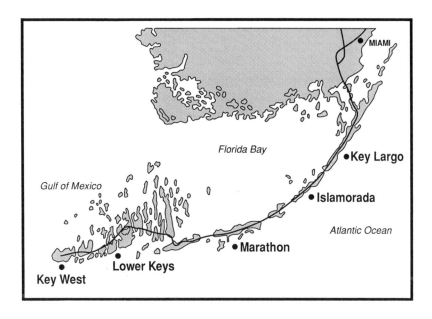

This unique adventure might most accurately be described as a shark hunt as opposed to a shark dive since sharks are not guaranteed. However, though they do usually show up about 70 percent of the time, enough for the dive to be held an average of once or twice a month at a cost of $250 per person with a four diver minimum.

If sharks aren't your thing, you can always pretend to be one of the bad guys chasing James Bond in a sleek yellow Perry submarine. Conch Republic also has the Keys only such sub and uses it to transport divers to remote reefs and wrecks once the dive boat has towed it to deep water. The sub isn't always in motion: if divers see something they want to get out to explore, the operator stops, rests the sub on the sand and divers do their thing.

For complete information, contact Conch Republic Divers, Inc. at Mile Marker 90.3, Plantation Key; 305/852-1655.

Don't Beach On The Reef

If you're piloting your own craft, be aware that destruction of coral formations in the Key Largo or Looe Key National Marine Sanctuaries either by grounding or improper anchoring can result in fines up to $50,000.

23

Therefore, keep the following in mind whenever you're navigating away from a marked channel:

Brown, Brown, Run Aground - coral formations make the water appear brown. Avoid these areas to keep from running aground.

Green, Green, Nice And Clean - indicates a clear sand bottom or beds to turtle grass which grow behind and around reefs. Be careful of these grass beds, vital to the fishery.

Blue, Blue Sail On Through - indicates deep, obstruction-free water. However, coral reefs can rise rapidly to the surface, so always keep a sharp lookout.

Stalking The Wily Lobster

Locating lobsters can be a lot like finding a needle in a haystack. In both instances you rely on eyesight instead of feel, or the search could be painful. Realizing its appeal is more than shell deep, the lobster has adopted the policy of many movie stars and taken to a sheltered reclusive life. As a result, snorkelers and divers will usually find lobster fairly difficult to locate. Normally, all you see are the thin waving antennae protruding from under ledges, crevices and holes and reef caves.

The southern lobster, *"Panulirus argus,"* as it is formally known, is quite distinctive in its lack of claws, a prominent feature much coveted on its northern counterpart. Most commonly the southern lobster is known as spiny lobster, receiving the name from the many sharp spines which protrude along his sides and the spiny-looking antennae. They can be found from Palm Beach County southward through the Keys and as far north as Daytona Beach.

During the day they are normally located around reefs; they also reside around jetties and artificial reefs made of old cars or tires. Since artificial reefs are visited mostly by line fishermen, they can be well worth regular weekday visits when angling activity is minimal.

In shallow water you can cover considerable lobster territory by dragging a snorkeler slowly behind a boat. Then, when a lobster is spotted, you simply let go and descend to capture your meal.

The first time you spot a lobster, the natural urge is to grab the ends of the openly exposed antennae. That's fine if all you want is a matched set of antennae, which are too delicate to endure much manhandling and normally break off.

Locating lobsters can be a lot like finding a needle in a haystack. In both instances you rely on eyesight instead of feel, or the search could be painful.

The spiny lobster is not only a delicacy, it is delicate and must be handled properly after capture to prevent spoilage. It should be kept cool in some way, either immediately put on ice, in a wet burlap sack or, best yet, in a refrigerator. Lobsters, like crabs, can sometimes be kept alive for several days in a refrigerator or ice chest. Once a lobster dies, it should be cooked immediately or the tail removed. This last point is crucial if the lobster is to be kept from spoiling.

Lobster Laws

Florida's lobster laws were in a state of transition as this book went to press. Lobster season normally runs from August through March. The state was proposing a special period for divers only on Wednesday and Thursday prior to August 1. This would be in addition to the federal sport season held the last full weekend before August 1. In order to alleviate pressure in the Keys, bag limits for the first day were suggested at 12 outside the Keys but 6 per day in Keys waters. Florida's marine fisheries laws are in constant flux these days, so be sure to check locally.

25

Because of heavy lobstering pressure each year, the size of the average legal lobster is only a pound. The law says a legal lobster is one with a carapace of more than three inches, measured from the depression behind the eye horns to the rear edge where it joins the tail. Unless you're eating on board, tail and carapace are not supposed to be separated until you return to shore. Once wrung, a legal tail is supposed to measure six inches from the top of the shell to the tip of the tail fin.

No egg bearing females can be taken. Grains, spears, grabs and hooks are prohibited. These laws are subject to change at anytime, so always check locally before you reach for that first lobster.

It's a $50 fine for minor lobster law violations, but a flagrant violation (or repeat offenses) can cost up to $1,000 and 120 days in jail. The court also has the authority to order an offender to forfeit his boat, dive gear and perhaps even his car.

One of the worst things to get caught doing is stealing lobsters from a commercial trap. If the law catches you it's a minimum of $250. If the lobsterman catches you, it could be a bullet. That's no exaggeration.

3

UNLOCKING THE UPPER KEYS

Tim takes us on an odyssey through the world's most-visited underwater playground

Including both Key Largo and Islamorada, this is the region most divers visit and where the majority of facilities are located. It's also home to John Pennekamp State Park, the world's first underwater park, and the Key Largo National Marine Sanctuary, which extends offshore protection farther than the state's three-mile limit.

It's the National Marine Sanctuary and not Pennekamp that actually protects the core dive reefs of the Upper Keys, including Molasses and French Reefs, Grecian Rocks, Key Largo Dry Rocks and more, a 20-mile-long segment showcasing Florida's most popular diving. In the past, however, most of the publicity went to Pennekamp after that state park was established in 1960. Then, in 1975, the national marine sanctuary status was added by the Secretary of Commerce, but Pennekamp Park personnel supervised the marine sanctuary until 1984, when NOAA began managing sanctuary territory.

The National Marine Sanctuary has been instrumental in helping reduce reef abuse through its system of Mooring Buoys (aiming for a total of 200) designed to eliminate anchors. The buoys are available to anyone on a first-come basis. For complete information, contact the Key Largo National Marine Sanctuary at 305/451-1644.

● One of the northernmost points is Carysfort Reef, easily identifiable by its 125-foot-tall lighthouse. (LORAN 14160.4/62211.9) Depths here plunge to as much as 100 feet or more, but the shallows have acres and acres of staghorn coral and tame tropical fish which sometimes can be fed by hand, so you'll find many good snorkeling spots here, too. Mooring Buoys C1-6 are on the ocean side of the light; C7-11 are behind a shallow reef on the shore side.

● To the south, the Elbow with its 36-foot high light tower with the No. 6 has large stands of elkhorn coral and lots of wreckage. An interesting artifact site is marked on most maps as "boilers;" it's also referred to locally as the Civil War Wreck. Little is left except for the steel parts. You can often spot lobster here early in the season, though they get picked out fast. The wreck, combined with the elkhorn corals, makes this a favorite photography site. (LORAN 14148.6/62229.3) The Mooring Buoys are marked E1-9.

● The Key Largo Dry Rocks is the location of the famed Christ of the Deep statue standing in about 25 feet of water. A heading of approximately 073 degrees from Marker 2 at the inlet to the park marina should put you over the statue. Locating it when coming in from other directions may not be as easy, so it pays to scan ahead with glasses. (LORAN 14143.0/62241.4) A large cordon of boats usually occupy the numerous Mooring Buoys as the day progresses.

The shallow water is ideal for snorkelers to prowl the tops of the reefs and still have a fine view of the statue. At the same time scuba divers, regardless of experience, will find this an active spot for exploration or photography. The nine-foot-high Christ, with arms upraised, is a duplicate of the statue by Italian sculptor Guido Galleti. His statue was placed in the Mediterranean near Genoa in 1954. Cast from the same mold, it weighs 4,000 pounds and stands on a 20-ton concrete base 7-1/2 feet tall and 11 feet square.

The statue was given to the Underwater Society of America by Italian industrialist Egidi Cressi to show his esteem for American underwater sportsmen. Cressi requested the statue be placed where it would not be commercialized or cheapened. The statue was a gift from the Underwater Society to the Florida Park Board. The statue with its upraised arms is intended to symbolize peace and understanding in the same way as the Christ of the Andes in South

Coral reefs and sponges are favorite photography subjects.

America. It is probably the most photographed underwater monument in the world.

The statue is only one attraction at this spot. Magnificent brain corals abound here, many of them unusually large. Also, there are huge stands of fire coral very near the surface. Fire coral is easy to recognize. It is a mustard color, usually growing in plate shape, with a white bordering. The sting from this coral can be vicious, as bad as a wasp's. Any area of the body marked by the coral should be cleaned with soap and water to get rid of the mucous-like secretion, then treated with a first-aid ointment, household ammonia or a paste of baking soda.

You will occasionally find some large barracuda here, which are so accustomed to photographers they have become totally blase about strobe flashes. Visibility at the statue may deteriorate according to the wind conditions. For serious photographers, this is not the finest spot which could have been chosen for sinking the statue. Accessibility seems to have been more important than diveability.

● About 3/4 of a mile S/SW of the Christ statue is Grecian Rocks, partially awash at low tide. The dense stand of elkhorn coral runs north-south for a half-mile and 150 yards in width. With depths of 4 to 25 feet, this is one of the best snorkeling areas in the area. (LORAN: 14141.2/62243.) Mooring Buoys are numbered G1-12.

● French Reef, 1 mile NE of Molasses Reef, is known for its coral caves and overhangs and the resident grouper that can be hand-fed. The caves are interesting photo props and you can never tell what you might find, including large green morays. Grunts, copper sweepers and yellowtail snapper all school here. Because of the many dark crevices, a flashlight is a good idea even in daylight to appreciate all the marine life. (LORAN 14129.6/62260.2)

The French Reef Mooring Buoys, F1-17, also help locate some of the better dive sites. If it's available, tie off at F1. Hourglass Cave is 50 feet shoreward from F1, while a 100-foot undercut with two swim-through passages is just off to the northeast. F3 marks the 20-foot tunnel Christmas Tree Cave, named after the colorful worms that grow here. F6 also has another swim-through under a coral ridge, located about 25 feet shoreward. At F7, follow the coral ridge northwest 100 feet to find an old anchor embedded in the coral.

● The best old wreck in the sanctuary is the "Benwood," not far from French Reef. The 350-foot British freighter was torpedoed in 1942 during World War II. This was truly a doomed ship: while heading to shallower water to accommodate planned salvage operations, the "Benwood" was rammed by another ship, this one supposedly friendly. For a time it was used as target practice, then the bow was blown up because it was a navigational hazard. Today, the wreck is scattered all over the bottom, its hull open and the deck plates resting flat on the sand. Lots of large fish such as grouper often hide out here. (LORAN: 14132.9/62254.3) The Benwood has 4 Mooring Buoys, B1-4.

The "Benwood" may be a disappointment if you've been conditioned by Hollywood to expect all sunken ships to still be whole and intact--with dark passageways to explore, portholes to swim through--everything left to show what the ship was once like. Instead, the "Benwood" looks like a junk pile. No thought was given to its esthetic appearance when it was dynamited.

Hidden away in the coral and fan encrusted remains of the pretzeled Benwood are some of the larger fish not easily seen at many of the other places: grouper, snook and barracuda all live here, not in obvious schools but in hidden isolation. You have to be patient in searching them out. A light is often helpful in some of the darker recesses of the wreck.

Since the "Benwood" is a moderate dive of about 50 feet, it's always been surprising to me to find snook here. I've normally associated these fighters with shallower water. Yet on several occasions I've seen a number of large snook at the edge of the wreck. One was close to 20 pounds, perhaps more. A dedicated inshore angler would have gone wild.

● Until part of it was damaged by an errant oil tanker in 1984, Molasses Reef was considered to be the best example of reef life anywhere in the Keys. With 25 different Mooring Buoys, only M11 & M12 are close to the damaged region. The other sections are still loaded with elkhorn and staghorn and brain corals and many, many kinds of tropicals. The best diving is around buoys M1-8 on the SE side of the 45-foot high steel light tower. Snorkelers generally use the shallower north end; deep dives are best off the south end, particularly Mooring Buoys M21-23. (LORAN: 14124.9/62268.5)

The fish on Molasses are fed so regularly by divers they have become quite tame. Some of the angelfish, in fact, come in so close in their search for a hand-out it's difficult to get a picture of anything but their open mouths. Tough problem! Most of Molasses Reef is less than 40 feet deep, so it's easy and safe diving except in high seas. Water here is often clearer than at other sites because of its nearness to the Gulf Stream. At the same time, its location makes it an easy boat ride, so Molasses tends to be the most crowded site of any in the sanctuary. Weekends can be murderous. The night diving is superb.

● Veteran divers familiar with the Keys' usual sights may wish to head to one of the two Coast Guard cutters sunk as artificial reefs near the southern end of the sanctuary in 1987. Besides providing new sightseeing areas, these artificial reefs help relocate some of the diving pressure from other sites. The 327-foot long, 2600-ton cutter "Duane" rests in 120 feet of water, but it sits upright vertically so the deck is at only about 50 feet. The compass heading is 190 degrees from Molasses Tower; LORAN 14122.2/62270.9. At 185 degrees from the Molasses Tower and in 130 feet of water is the cookie-cutter twin, the 327-foot long, 2600-ton "Bibb." Since the

31

ship rests on its starboard side, it's a deeper swim to the "Bibb;" 95 feet to the railing on the port side, the shallowest part available (LORAN: 14122.9/62270.3).

Deliberately placed farther offshore than any of the reefs in order not to impede boat traffic, the "Duane" and "Bibb" are subject to occasional currents which can make safe diving impossible. That is not the case most of the time; still, always go down the anchor rope and swim against the current. Lights are needed to thoroughly explore the superstructures, which were left open to divers.

● Nine other artificial reefs also have been created through the auspices of the Florida Keys Artificial Reef Association, Inc., for a total of 11. Most are farther south from Marathon to Key West, but traveling for 2.6 nautical miles from Islamorada's Alligator Light will put you on five different structures intended to create a single artificial reef system. It includes old bridges, a 120-foot long steel barge and the "Eagle," a 287-foot freighter. Bottom depth is 120 to 110 feet, though the "Eagle" rises 50 feet off the bottom. The other structures extend only 10 to 15 feet high. Anyone wishing to help the non-profit Florida Keys Artificial Reef Association is encouraged to send donations to P.O. Box 917, Big Pine Key, FL 33043.

Treasure Fleet

Ever dream of finding bars of gold or silver on the ocean floor? It's possible--though very unlikely--you might be lucky enough to do just that on the Spanish treasure fleet littered between Key Largo and Key Vaca (near Marathon) by a hurricane on September 15, 1733. The Spaniards salvaged what they could off the 21 ships and modern treasure hunters also have had a go.

Yet some believe the bulk of the treasure is still there, buried under the coral and sands. Fanning the sand around the wrecks still yields pottery and pewter. Silver is also sometimes found.

The following eight galleons all lie in 18-35 feet of water, plenty shallow for long lengths of bottom time. On some you could spend literally the whole day, sucking tank after tank, and never have to worry about decompressing. Ballast stone is the most obvious underwater marker at all these sites:

There are 822 islands in the Keys chain large enough to be recorded on government charts, scores more of tiny mangrove clumps too small to be included. Only about 30 are inhabited. They extend for 120 miles, bounded by the Atlantic on the east and the Gulf of Mexico on the west, to form the southernmost point in the continental U.S.

● "Infante," LORAN 14109.0/43266.0, just 75 yards southeast of Little Conch Reef. Known for its "pillar dollars," silver coins with special edge markings.

● "San Jose," LORAN 14108.5/43268.8, about 1 mile east of Little Conch Reef. The ribs and keel are exposed. At least $30,000 was removed from here in 1973.

● "El Capitan," LORAN 14103.18/43276.5, 6 miles E-SE of Windley Key. Another ballast pile that still yields some exciting finds.

● "Chaves," LORAN 14098.5/43292.7, just off Windley Key. In only 10 feet of water.

● "Herrera," 2-1/2 miles south of Snake Creek Bridge in an 18-foot deep grass bed. Clay figurines have been one of the most intriguing retrievals.

● "Tres Puentes," LORAN 14093.5/43296.5, 3-1/2 miles south-southeast of Snake Creek Bridge. Best finds have been on the ocean side of the ballast pile.

● "San Pedro," LORAN 14082.2/43320.8, 1-1/4 miles south of Indian Key. Another grass bed that has yielded many coins, mostly on the ocean side.

● "Lerri," LORAN 14077.3/43330.6, 3/4 of a mile off Lower Matecumbe. Few coins to date but you may find other relics.

Dive Into History

Islamorada is perhaps the only place in North America where divers can investigate and aid in the preservation of ancient Spanish galleons. Through a unique program called "Dive Into History," underwater archaeologist R. Duncan Mathewson III is attempting to enhance the diving appeal of historically significant wrecks of ancient Spanish galleons for sport divers and snorkelers. Mathewson's program emphasizes ecotourism, activities in which visitors observe the Keys' extremely fragile environment without having any adverse impact.

The San Pedro Underwater Archaeological Preserve in 18-foot deep waters oceanside off Indian Key was the initial site for an underwater classroom. The San Pedro was part of the ill-fated 21-ship Spanish fleet in which all but one of the boats were destroyed by a deadly storm that scattered the wrecks along 80 miles of Keys bottom. It happened on a truly unlucky Friday 13, in July of 1733.

On Mathewson's program, divers do not mine the wrecks for artifacts but instead help in restoring and measuring wreck sites which may contain a tremendous wealth of historical value.

The San Pedro site is shallow enough that both snorkelers and divers can view the seven concrete cannon replicas, ballast rock and even limited remains of the wooden hull. The 500-pound cannons were placed in their historically accurate position as part of the "Dive Into History" program.

"These are the Keys' oldest artificial reefs," points out John Ovitt of the World Down Under Dive Shop at Cheeca Lodge in Islamorada which conducts most but not all of the trips.

Ovitt says a no-fishing policy is strictly enforced at the San Pedro site, where "there is a tremendous amount of marine life."

The "Dive Into History" program is held only about once a month, so it's necessary to plan ahead. Contact the World Down Under at 305/664-2777.

4

MIDDLE & LOWER KEYS
DISCOVERIES

Some of Tim's favorite underwater photography sites.

With all there is to see and do in the Upper Keys, why go anywhere else? In truth, the majority of divers never venture farther south into the Middle Keys or Key West. Those who do tend to be searching for something different (though not necessarily better) underwater or on land.

The Marathon area, 80 miles from the mainland and 50 miles above Key West, is second largest to Key West. Marathon also has its own small airport. That means that those who want to fly/drive and dive can hop from Miami to Marathon and totally avoid the Upper Keys if they wish.

Regrettably, much of the Middle Keys are developing so that before much longer it will look like everywhere else with shopping malls and pricey resorts. The Middle Keys technically start at Long Key State Park, which has the finest ocean-front camping in all of the Keys. Surrounded by tall, shady Australian pines and bordered by an ocean-front beach, the 60 camp sites offer the stereotypical vision many visitors have of the Keys and its beaches but rarely find. Good beaches in the Keys are few because the soil consists primarily of a thin organic layer over rocky limestone. So if camping while diving is a priority, the 1,000-acre Long Key park should be a first choice.

Bonefish, tarpon and barracuda fishing is also particularly good here. Zane Grey Creek, which starts in Long Key park, was named after the famed western author who fished here regularly. Henry Flagler, the same railroad empire magnate who transformed St. Augustine into a popular winter retreat for the rich, also built a fish camp on Long Key to attract elite anglers: Zane Grey was but one of many who came to test the waters, liked what he found and returned regularly.

● One of the better shallow dive spots in the Middle Keys, despite its grisly name, is Coffins Patch, about 3-1/2 miles from Key Colony Beach. With huge brain corals, sizable stands of staghorn and numerous ledges, you'll often see lobster and large schools of French grunts and mutton snapper here.

● The 200-foot steel vessel "Thunderbolt," about a mile south-southwest of Marker 20, was deliberately sunk in 1986 to start an artificial reef program in the Middle Keys. Sitting upright in 115 feet, it still contains two bronze propellers and an intact bridge, only 75 feet from the surface. A great photo opportunity. (LORAN: 14034.0/43403.4)

● Delta Shoals, about 1-1/2 miles east-northeast of Sombrero Light, runs for 1/2-mile east and west. Depths are shallow, only 10-20 feet. Best diving is on the oceanside, which includes several very old wrecks, none known to have had treasure. One is called the "Ivory Wreck" because of the elephant tusks found on it.

● Sombrero Reef, 8 miles southwest of Key Colony Beach, couldn't be easier to find, it has a 142-foot-high light tower. Depths range to only about 30 feet, yet the bottom is scalloped with sand ravines and high coral cliffs. You will find lots of sea fans here as well as some of the prettiest tropicals of all, including the dazzling jewelfish which sparkles in its multi-shades of blue.

Explore Looe Key N.M.S.

Many consider the Looe Key National Marine Sanctuary, six miles south of Big Pine Key, to have the finest coral and fish collection outside of Key Largo/Islamorada. The Looe Key Sanctuary, covering 5.3 sq. miles of federal waters, is named after the 44-gun British frigate "HMS Looe" which sank on the reef in 1744. This sanctuary also employs Mooring Buoys on a first-come

Friendly grouper are a common sight in the Keys.

basis. Actually situated off Big Pine Key, most access is from Marathon. For information, call the sanctuary offices at 305/872-4039. Looe Key National Marine Sanctuary boundries: Northwest corner LORAN 13972.8/43538.6, Northwest corner LORAN 13979.4/43523.9.

The spur and groove formation of Looe Key, so classic throughout most of the Keys, is well illustrated at Looe Key Reef. Ballast stone and the anchor still remain, but it may be difficult to distinguish the relics from the coral. No wreck picking is permitted since this is a sanctuary.

Looe Key Reef, about 800 yards long and 200 yards wide, provides more than enough activity to keep a diver occupied for days. Staghorn, elkhorn, flower, star, brain--all the corals are here in this compact area. In addition, there are also the remains of other wrecks scattered throughout the reef. The "Looe" itself is believed to be in the south central portion. This is an excellent spot for night diving, when the marine life with easy to find in fairly shallow water (15 to 30 feet deep).

Brittle stars, octopus and numerous other species make excellent macro-photography subects after dark. Since Looe Key is partially awash, there is always a leeward side for diving in most normal wind conditions. This is not the case in many places farther north where the wind often determines where--and if--you dive.

Mooring Buoys 1-32 near the reef core are some of the best coral formations, the beautiful coral fingers that bottom at 30 feet deep. Buoys 33-39 are good snorkeling spots on the shore side of the reef, with depths of only 3-15 feet. A mile north of Marker 24, buoys 40-49 are over patch reefs that average 16 feet deep. Visibility is not as good as on the outer reefs. Southwest of Marker 24, buoys 50-70 target the deeper waters. In the 30-70 foot zone, sponges and octocorals are quite thick while the hard corals are low profile. From 70-105 feet, the ledges and big rocks contain the most interesting sea life, including some surprisingly big fish.

No spearing is allowed inside Looe Key sanctuary, although line fishing is permitted. Lobstering is also permissible in season except in the core reef area marked off by four yellow buoys.

When the Atlantic is rough, the Content Keys on the Gulf side are usually protected on even the windiest days. Although not as good as the Atlantic side, they do assure Middle Keys diving virtually year-round.

● Fore Reef: Majestic slopes and ledges of living corals, supported by 7000 years of coral growth, form the classical spur and groove of three-dimension in living color, combined with the spectacular color and array of tropical fish, make this the most popular habitat among divers in the sanctuary. Finger-like coral spurs, separated by grooves of sand and coral rubble, have been formed as a result of seaward growth of Elkhorn coral. Depth of the spurs range from three feet along the shallow reef crest to 30 at their seaward extent.

● Rubble Zone: Fragments of coral rubble have been thrown behind the reef crest and distributed by currents and wave action over the centuries. The majority of the rubble that parallels the reef crest has been cemented together by various processes. This habitat is home to many organisms that will not be found anywhere else in the Sanctuary. Two horn-like extensions of the rubble zone extend shoreward at the western and eastern ends of the rubble ridge. These horns are situated in such a manner as to protect the Reef

Flat from prevailing winds. Although it's tempting, please do not stand up on the rubble; you may destroy new coral recruits that are not easily observed.

● Reef Flat: As a refuge from aid and wave action, the Reef Flat is the second most popular location in the Sanctuary. The area is 1 to 5m (3-15') deep and is primarily occupied by a seagrass bed composed of turtle and manatee grasses. Numerous algaes add to the diversity of plant life in this habitat. Novice snorklers often find this a relaxing location for their first open water dive, Careful and observant snorklers can observe marine life and fish cleaning behavior at many of the scattered coral reefs. Remember, the conch you may see in this area are protected.

● Patch Reef (Backreef): Located away from the Fore Reef, this habitat is often overlooked by most visitors to the Sanctuary. Lack of evidence as to its presence (except for dark patches on the bottom) have left this area virtually unexplored by recreational divers. Since the habitat is in close proximity to Hawk Channel, the visibility is sometimes poor. Marine life is diverse and abundant on the Patch Reefs. The benthic organisms are dominated by soft corals that may grow to as much as six feet tall. Numerous species of sponges and stony corals add to the beauty of this densely populated substrate. Other invertebrates, as well as many species of fish, use the habitat as refuge and add tremendously to it's splendor. Fisherman find this a very productive area.

● Intermediate Reef: An ancient , low profile spur and groove formation provides the primary substrate for this habitat. Located southwest of the Core Area, this area comprises the majority of reef substrate in the Sanctuary. Accessible to only more experienced SCUBA divers, this spectacular area begins in at 30 feet and extends out to 70. Enormous sponges, soft corals, and a deep water assemblage of stony corals dominate the sessile organisms of this habitat. Many of the coral and fishes found here are not common to other parts of the Sanctuary. Isolated patches of this bottom type are scattered to the west of the Core Area. This is preferred location for experienced recreational fishermen.

● Deep Reef: At a depth of approximately 70 feet the intermediate Reef begins to slope at a 30 degree angle to a depth of 105. The Deep Reef, as it is called, is strikingly different than any other part of the Sanctuary. Although much of the solid substrate observed here is barren and covered with sediment, there remains spectacular soft and stony coral colonies to appreciate. Many species of invertebrates and fishes can only be observed in this habitat. Only the most experienced SCUBA dives should attempt this dive.

● Sand Plain And Side Channels: Although the majority of the Sand Plain is uniformly flat and featureless, this vast portion of the Sanctuary should not be overlooked. Occasional outcroppings provide a habitat for a myriad of invertebrates and fish life, and these miniature "reefs" offer ideal captive subjects for underwater photography. The Sand habitat is home to many starfish, urchins, and mollusks that won't be observed anywhere else in the Sanctuary, and many species of fish spend the majority of their life cycle in the Sand Plains. Drift dives across the Sand Plains can add interest and versatility to ones' exploration of the total coral reef ecosystem.

Incidentally, the Seven Mile Bridge connecting Marathon with the Lower Keys is a favorite lobster hunting ground since the pilings of both the old and new bridges provide plenty of hiding places. You may also run across large tarpon, barracuda, grouper and possibly even a shark, particularly at night.

The Lower Keys

Florida's last uncharted dive destination begins south of Marathon and ends at Key West. In the Lower Keys, you can still find huge tracts of undeveloped land (huge for the Keys, anyway) on places like Big Pine Key, habitat for the rare and tiny Key Deer which can often be spotted early and late in the day. Many of the Lower Keys have been described as almost as pristine and beautiful as the day they were formed.

However, they all tend to be overshadowed by the ever increasing glitz of Key West, which in a few short years has turned itself into a major tourist destination. Some would argue that the shopping and resort selection virtually rivals that of Miami Beach, though certainly on a smaller scale.

A lot of the wonderful craziness of the old Key West days definitely is gone. It's doubtful that one of Key West's most famous residents, Ernest Hemingway, would want to live in the clamor and clutter of the modern city which attracts more than a million people annually.

The Dry Tortugas are inaccessible and a rather long voyage; the reefs surrounding Fort Jefferson are mostly virgin and unspoiled.

Besides being the southern-most point in the U.S., Key West is the land of perpetual sunsets. Sunset watching has become an important ritual, luring hundreds of visitors and a score of street performers to the Mallory Dock area about an hour before darkness. It's a combination festival and freak show as contortionists, bag pipe players and astrologers all try to hussle a living off the tourists. Dining and nighttime activitites are at their most varied and sophisticated in Key West. You can enjoy everything from gourment cuisine to Jimmy Buffet himself, the Keys' poet laureate, who occasionally shows up in town.

Most divers don't make it was far as Key West. They allow themselves to be lured into the water many miles farther north in order to save on travel time. Yet Key West diving easily matches that found around Key Largo and is somewhat surer; when the Atlantic is acting up, there is still the shallow Gulf side and its many wrecks.

And for divers who want something resembling big-city nightlife, Key West if the best place around for it. There are museums and other attractions to keep non-diving family members occupied during the day while you're out over the reefs doing your own thing.

Not having the benefit of a government agency governing any of the inshore waters, Key West divers have to rely on a private non-profit organization called Reef Relief. It has been placing Mooring Buoys off Key West since 1988. Membership is available by writing Reef Relief, 1223 Royal Street, Key West, FL 33040.

One of the most visited sites is Western Sambo reef. Stretching over a mile and with depths from 30 to over 100 feet, this site is particularly well known for its shelling. It's kind of an underwater version of Sanibel Island. Helmet conchs and flamingo tongues have been common items here in the past. Go four miles south of Boca Chica Channel to black & white buoy No. 2. Due east is a pole marking the tip of Western Sambo. Eastern and Middle Sambos are also here, separated by sandy deserts. Depths are only 10-40, so it's easy to spot coral formations from your boat.

A half mile south of Western Sambo is the "Aquanaut," a 50-foot wooden tug in only 75 feet. Sunk in 1967, this is one of the area's easiest wreck dives. A mile southwest of Western Sambo is the Ten Fathom Ledge. The ocean side, which drops from 50 to 115 feet, can be an exciting drift dive.

The shallow reef area (15-30 feet) called Nine Foot Stake is a regular testing ground for the Navy; located a mile west of Marker No. 1. Sand Key, six miles south of Key West, has a 110-foot tall lighthouse marking it, so the reef is quite easy to find. This is a good all-around spot for both snorkeling and scuba. The bottom varies from 15 to 70 feet. The coral ledges and caves down deeper often contain a fair number of grouper.

The Ten Fathom Bar, 1/2-mile south of Sand Key, has remarkably clear water much of the year. An unusual wall dive, the reef starts at 25 feet and drops to 130. Strong current is often encountered the first 30 feet; go hand over hand down the anchor line. Lots of tame snapper and grouper. Head 4-1/2 miles south of Sand Key Light to reach the Ten Fathom Ledge off the Western Dry Rocks, one of the best spots of all for reef diving. Depths are shallow, only 40-50 feet, and the water is unusually clear because of the Gulf Stream.

Smith Shoal has everything a good dive site should have, except for clear water. Located 12 miles northwest of Key West and

Marine life is diverse and abundant on the Patch Reefs.

marked with a 47-foot tower, visibility is only around 20 feet, but it does have lots of big stands of brain and staghorn corals. Head on a 293-degree course and run seven miles from the Smith Shoal Tower to reach a group of wrecks dating back to the 1940s. Visibility can be a low 25 feet, but the chance to get close to large grouper, jewfish and cobia helps compensate.

On the Gulf side, the many shallow wreck sites require careful navigating to keep from running aground. These ships still have some decent artifacts, though most of the better items have long since been removed. You can often find large fish hiding here which are prime candidates for photography.

The best diving of all, however, is another 60 miles south of Key West in the Dry Tortugas. A number of charter boats run dives regularly from both Key West and Marathon. They normally last as long as a week. The Tortugas reefs are protected, just like Pennekamp's, but they suffer none of the same over-population problems.

As the Dry Tortugas are continually bathed by the warm clear waters of the Gulf Stream, visibility ranges 80 to 100 feet most of the year. Since it is so inaccessible and a rather long voyage, the reefs there for the most part are as they were hundreds of years ago; virgin and unspoiled.

Because of the distance and the fact none of the reefs are marked, this is a trip best made in the company of those on a chartered dive boat. Otherwise, you could spend days diving the place and still miss the better reefs and wrecks. The Dry Tortugas are likely to remain Florida's last uncharted dive location.

5

BONEFISH AND PERMIT FLATS

Tim challenges the gray ghosts of the flats.

The bonefish raced away out of control, the pink jig firmly clamped in his mouth. I watched the line feed out at an unbelievable speed, 100 feet of 6-lb. test monofilament stripped off in the wink of an eye. Unable to stop the fish's progress, I held on helplessly, like a rider on horseback bounced out of his stirrups.

All I could do was stand still, my rod raised high, and wait for the fish to tire. In the meantime, it was as if I had hooked on to a passing powerboat going full throttle.

My ultra-light spinning rod danced and bent like a divining rod gone mad. The line was so tight and strained from the fish's continual pull that it hummed dangerously in the wind, almost ready to part.

It was wonderful. Pound for pound, on light tackle, nothing else that swims off Islamorada in the Florida Keys can match the power of a bonefish.

But all good things eventually end, even a bonefish's incredible stamina. Five minutes later I boated the exhausted fish, swimming on its side. The six-pound bone had fought like a freshwater fish twice that size. As soon as we released it, my guide returned to the high platform of the shallow draft skiff and continued to pole us over the clear water flats.

However, you don't need a boat to locate bonefish. Almost all the oceanside flats from Key Biscayne to the tip of the Keys are prime territory. You can locate bonefish by quietly stalking from shore and simply wading the flats. Or you can hire a qualified guide to find them for you with his boat. It all depends on how much time, and money, you can invest in this quest.

Bonefish are literally everywhere throughout the Keys, although most anglers concentrate their search from Islamorada down to the Big Pine region. Because of their tenacious strength and the challenge it takes to catch them, dedicated anglers from around the country trek to the Florida Keys annually to try their skill.

Bonefishing is unique in that your hook never touches the water until you first spot the fish you want to cast to. Your casts must be precisely aimed, placed just beyond and in front of the fish, so the lure can be slowly retrieved across the fish's path. Put the lure too far beyond and a bonefish will swim by without seeing it. Plop it on top of him and he'll spook, disappearing instantly.

Such precision casting definitely requires some previous skill with a fly or spinning rod. It also helps to have strong nerves to bolster yourself each time the fish and lure make their close encounter. If the fish passes up the lure (as he usually does), it's try, try again.

On occasion, hooking a bonefish can be relatively easy if the fish are in the mood to eat and you tip your jig with a piece of shrimp as an added enticement. But most often, bonefish are unbelievably wary and easily spooked. They seem to live in a constant state of alarm. I've known periods when all the fish were so wary they would vanish from sight before the lure even hit the water.

Such is the challenging unpredictability of bonefishing.

In terms of looks, the bonefish is flashy: his elongated torpedo shape has bright silver scales that may also have hues of pearl and blue-green. Its small mouth, located under a piglike snout, is used for grubbing the bottom for crabs and other crustaceans. When feeding nose down in shallow flats, a bonefish's tail is often visible as it breaks the water. This behavior, known as tailing, is one of the first things a guide looks for when scanning the flats.

Although greatly sought, bonefish are only for sport, not eating. As their name implies, they are far too bony for most people's taste.

Most oceanside flats from Key Biscayne to the tip of the Keys are prime bonefish territory.

As in deep sea fishing, the person most responsible for a successful bonefishing trip is the guide. Through his long years of experience, he is the one who knows on which flats the fish will be according to how high or low the tide. More importantly, he has the ability to spot fish that most anglers never see. The extreme glare that bounces off the water can be an impenetrable fog, even for those wearing the mandatory polarized sunglasses that helps reduce it. The majority of anglers simply never see the dark torpedo shapes swimming over the sand until their guide points them out.

But a good guide can pick out a bonefish from among the eel grass and other bottom cover from as much as 30 yards away. With

47

Backcountry Bones Tips

"OK! We have fresh muds right here ... look at them ... there's three of them! Dammit where did they come from? There's four or five of them! See them going? See the shadow?" guide Gary Ellis' voice urgently pointed out the ghost-like shapes in the three-foot-deep flat. "He's coming for it, that bonefish is coming toward your bait! Oh no, he's spooked!"

An angler can't control when a bonefish will strike. However, Ellis, a Keys bonefish guide for more than 20 years, shares some techniques that can help your chances.

● **Looking for Bones** - Use a scanning pattern. Using the bow of the boat as 12 o'clock, scan out to 1 o'clock, back to the boat and then out again to 2 o'clock and back to the boat and then out to 3 o'clock, etc.

"It is difficult, but you must learn to spot bonefish," explains Ellis. "Just practice, and it goes without saying that you need polarized sunglasses."

Scanning is also an excellent way to communicate with your guide. "I always have the angler point the rod tip to the spot that he thinks I'm talking about," says Ellis. "Then I can adjust his line of sight to where the fish are."

● **Best Baits** - Ellis believes that nothing beats live shrimp.

"If the water is calm, I prefer to use a single hook. I bend it a little so that the shrimp makes it weedless," he explains. "If it's windy, then I rig a shrimp on a 1/4 oz. jig with a 4/0 hook for better casting control. The choppy waters will keep the noise down when the bait lands."

● **Tackle** - Use very sharp hooks. "Only the sharpest hook will get into that bony mouth," he explains. "I also use barbless hooks. I don't worry so much about the hook coming out, I'm more worried about the hook going in through the armor. It's your angling ability that will keep the hook from popping out." Light line, 8 to 10 pound, is recommended, and absolutely no leader. "Even a Bimini twist knot can be seen by the skittish bonefish."

● **Casting Technique** - The one thing that determines your success is casting technique. A cast lobbed very high will plop loudly on the surface and spook the bones. Casting too close to the fish will also spook them, and casting too far will make the bones totally miss the bait.

"The ideal scenario is to cast very softly in front of a bonefish and let him swim to the bait," explains Ellis. "Hold the rod tip down and give him a couple of seconds to swallow it. Then just give it a jerk or two. If he drops the bait, a soft jerk will just place it a short distance where the bone can still retrieve it."

Gary Ellis likes to share many other bonefish techniques with his clients while fishing around Islamorada. His phone number is 305/664-8452.

-- Lilliam Morse Larsen

Precision casting is definitely required for successful bonefishing, as well as some previous skill with a fly or spinning rod.

spooky bonefish, anglers must cast from extreme distances; precision casting becomes next to impossible when you can't see the fish.

A good guide is capable of talking an angler into making a winning cast with instructions like "Bonefish at two o'clock, 10 yards out." Of course, the bonefish is apt to be unappreciative of all such efforts and pass the lure by.

At high tide the water may be too deep for even the guide to see fish. That's the time to "fish the muds." Muds occur when bonefish school together to feed. Their bottom grubbing discolors the water, making it more of a milky white instead of a dark blue. A fresh mud is a floating marker that says "Fish here!" A mud left by feeding bonefish may extend a hundred yards, and the size often indicates the number of fish in the school.

Once a mud is sighted, the boat drifts through it as the anglers cast into the freshest area. This is not a method that works well for fly fishermen, who are better able to cast by wading the flats.

Although the Keys are the best known location, Biscayne Bay near Miami is also has a reputation for unusually large fish. Biscayne bones weighing over eight pounds are for the serious angler who is most concerned about the quality size of his fish, not the quantity.

To book a guide for Key Biscayne, contact Chief's Bait & Tackle, 20 W. McIntyre St., Key Biscayne, FL 33149; (305) 361-2499. To fish the Islamorada area, contact Bud & Mary's Fishing Marina, MM 795., Islamorada, FL 33036; (305) 664-2461. Also Holiday Isle Resort & Marina, MM84, Islamorada; 305/664-2321. Between them, the two Keys marinas have a list of over 50 guides who specialize in bonefishing.

It's possible to spend a couple of days seeking bonefish and yet never land one. If that happens, don't give up. The satisfaction of seeking and ultimately landing one of these sleek silver torpedoes is what bonefishing is all about.

Permit, Me!

Now, here is a fish to truly rejoice over if he happens to take your lure. As hard-fighting as bonefish and tarpon are, ounce for ounce the permit has them both beat. Permit, which range between 10-40 pounds, may demand as much as three hours of hard fighting on light tackle. Permit never quit.

The Atlantic permit, sometimes called great pompano, is present throughout the Keys, but they are seldom seen. Bonefish are hookhogs in comparison. The greatest concentration of permit appears to be from the Middle Keys, south. The Content Keys are especially noted for their large numbers of permit. In the past, lucky anglers have been able to see as many as a hundred in a day. Even in such excellent circumstances, it seems you hook only one fish for every three-score you see.

Permit are not as visible because they spend a great deal of time in holes and channels and, like bones, come up on the flats at flood tide. However, because permit are so deep bodied, they require twice as much water as a bonefish before they make their flats entry. You can usually spot their tails and dorsals breaking the surface when the fish are feeding. Smaller permit usually travel in schools, while larger fish tend to be loners.

6

THE MIAMI WRECKS

Tim shows wreck divers where to overdose in Dade County

This may come as a surprise to you--it certainly did to me--but Dade County has more diveable sunken ships than anywhere else in the world except for Truk Lagoon, a major World War II battleground.

Where Truk's wrecks date back to 1944, all of Dade County's ships have been sunk since 1981 as part of their Artificial Reef Program.

The sea is just like the land: devoid of permanent residents except in those rare places where shelter and food are readily available. It requires structure of some kind-- whether a natural reef, cast-off debris, a sunken ship or whatever-- to provide these essential factors.

Miami's artificial reef program has created a new dive industry and fisheries resource that did not exist before. For instance, in 1980, only one dive boat operated out of Miami; today, there are a dozen or more, and virtually all make the wrecks their primary destination.

The greater Miami area, which has more divers on a per capita basis than anywhere else in the country, has finally turned into a dive destination in itself. Ironically, the visitors who now come to dive the wrecks also discover just how good diving some of the reefs are,

51

one of those startling new developments which a few locals knew all along.

Because the conditions of Miami's blue-green water are not all that different from those in the Keys, Dade County's reefs tend to be more developed and hold more abundant marine life than those limestone formations farther north.

Since 1985, more than 20 ships have been sunk in less than 100 feet of water. At the moment, Miami offers 11 different off-shore artificial reef sites, all of which contain multiple wrecks. The best diving is found in the five most accessible ones: Government Cut, Anchorage, Key Biscayne, R.J. Diving and Haulover.

In Key Biscayne alone, for example, you can dive the 105-foot long tug, "Rio Miami," sunk in 70 feet of water in 1989 during a segment on artificial reef building for the TV news show "20/20." Joining the "Rio Miami" is a three-ship package known as the "Belzona Triangle" named after the corporation which provided the funds that acquired the ships.

The marine growth on the older vessels is incredibly prolific and colorful. The ships are not merely bare metal hulks which are briefly dramatic when first seen from a distance. Instead, these ships are packed with far greater numbers of passengers than they could ever have held while afloat. A few are so encrusted they look like they have been down for decades.

Ben Mostkoff is the director of the Department of Environmental Resource Management (DERM), the agency in charge of finding and positioning the artificial reefs. Some of the wrecks, he explains, are deep enough to be only of interest to sport fishermen, not divers. In fact, the program initially was intended as a way to enhance the local fishery resource.

At present, DERM has placed over 500,000 cubic yards of reef material which includes 30 ships from 300 feet to 100 feet long and a couple of Tenneco Oil platforms. The oil platforms, located on the Dade/Broward County line, is the largest single artificial reef on the entire East Coast of the U.S. Most of the "shipreefs" came from the Miami River, which used to be flooded with abandoned vessels. Unfortunately, those have been used up so now DERM is relying on donated ships or buying confiscated vessels from the U.S. Coast Guard.

The S.S. Lowrance, a 435-foot freighter, is one of the largest artificial reefs on the East Coast.

Mostkoff says that using a ship is the most economical use of steel, concrete wood and fiberglass to form a substrate. When sunk at a depth shallow enough to permit sunlight penetration--water less than 100 feet deep--the ships provide the foundation for the marine growth which attaches to the vessel.

This new growth provides a food supply first for the juvenile fish that take up residence, then the larger species which arrive to take advantage of the newly created food chain.

"The artificial reef program simply speeds up the natural process. Nature provided rock outcroppings and hard bottom on which the natural reefs are occurring. We are providing the steel and concrete on which the artificial reefs develop.

"Over a period of about 20 years, a wreck duplicates a natural reef system. All we're doing is expediting nature," Mostkoff says.

After DERM acquires a ship, its first step is to clean up the vessel better than it was the first day it ever went to sea. That involves removing all the fuel, fluids, freons, hydrocarbons, anything not compatible with sea water, or anything that might float off (such as doors or cargo) to become a navigation hazard.

Depth is not the only consideration about where a wreck should be sunk. A critical step is the offshore biological survey -- the ship is placed on a barren sand bottom so it won't compete with any of the natural reef system.

A sinking is a long, elaborate affair, taking about 6 months from the time it's found until the time it's sunk. Each wreck requires the cooperation and coordination of the Metro-Dade bomb squad, U.S. Coast Guard and Florida Marine Patrol. The ship is anchored on a preselected site and carefully placed explosives send the ship down quickly so it will not drift away from the intended site.

Explosives are set up in four areas: bow, stern and two sections amid-ship. These are sand-blasted charges, which means bags of sand are placed on top of the dynamite so all the force is directed downwards. This approach usually causes the ships to flood evenly and go straight down; 90 percent of the time they settle perfectly, on the full length of their keel.

What was a barren underwater desert quickly transforms into a vibrant, lively community. Fish show up at the new reefs within hours of placement. It's believed the ships set up a pressure wave in the water column which helps the fish detect the vessel and they begin schooling first out of curiosity and remain because the artificial reef provides a perfect new home.

Algae growth, the first important element of the new reef system, appears within a few weeks, followed by the corals and sponges. Anywhere from six months to a year after sinking divers will find a new community that didn't exist before. The conditions get better and better every year, as new residents move in and old ones expand. Over-crowding on wrecks is something divers always like to see.

● The 200-foot freighter "Almarante" was one of the first artificial reefs. It sits in 130 feet of water off Elliott Key. It is heavily coral encrusted and alive with fish, particularly French angels, grunts and a roving patrol of barracuda. Also lots of beautiful gorgonian fans, colorful encrusting sponges, hyrdroids and ascidians. You should carry a flashlight, even in daytime, to appreciate the incredible colors growing on the open decks as well as in the hidden nooks and crannies.

● The "Ultra Freeze" was sent down in the summer of 1984. Bottoming out at 120 feet, she is one of the most popular deep dives. The top is as shallow as 70 feet. From the very beginning one of the wreck's main attractions has been a large school of horseye jacks.

When approaching fish schools on this or any other wreck, don't use quick jerky movements with your arms as you approach. You'll look menacing and threatening; the fish may mistake you for a predator and depart very quickly. Instead, glide or drift in on an imaginary flight path like an airplane landing smoothly on the deck of an aircraft carrier.

● The "Orion" was a tugboat that worked in the Panama Canal. Sunk in the early 1980s and still looking very much like a tugboat, it sits in 95 feet of water, listing slightly to starboard. You'll find a tremendous photo opportunity in the still intact wheelhouse. It's possible to swim through the entire ship, especially the holds usually filled with glassy sweepers. Like most Miami wrecks, it has several entrances and exits for divers and current to flow through.

● One of the oldest wrecks is the "Biscayne" in about 60 feet of water. It's one of the best known check-out dive sites for the whole of South Florida. Forty feet to the top of the deck, the water here is normally clear and calm. The big schools of fish are diver friendly, including morays that eat out of your hand. Because of its age, the "Biscayne" has an amazingly thick coating of coral and sponges, on par with more famous Caribbean wrecks such as the "Balboa" in Grand Cayman. The coral looks like it's been developing over decades, not just a matter of years. Divers are expected to treat this man-induced coral with as much consideration as a natural reef. That means no kicking, pulling or souvenir collecting.

● Another deep Miami wreck is the "Blue Fire," in 120 feet of water with 100 feet to the main deck. Very little to see on the sand areas around this or any of the ships. The best coral formation is always on the top deck. Schools of snapper often hover around the superstructure, which has fallen off to the side.

● The "Sarah Jane" is actually a group of wrecks assembled in the same area over the years. A main showpiece is a metal barge, but others are made of wood, which decompose fairly rapidly. Wooden wrecks also tend to attract a different type of fish and marine growth than metal-hulled vessels, which lose their high profile very quickly. At this site, you can cover four or five wrecks on a single dive, each quite different. Because they are relatively deep and rest close to the bottom, your dive time is limited.

● The "Belcher Barge," donated by the Belcher Oil Co., consists of huge concrete pipes and debris that has one of the largest collections of barracuda in the Miami area. In the winter, hundreds of barracudas will sometimes be stacked up from the sand all the way to the surface.

● The "Shamrock" is north of Government Cut, one of South Florida's main cruise ship channels. The tide flushes water northward out of Biscayne Bay through Government Cut, so wrecks north of the Cut develop differently. Not only is the water north of the Cut not as clear, the growth is faster and the fish life more concentrated. The concrete pipes around the Shamrock are one of the best spots for macro photography in all Miami.

● The "Police Barge" was unknown for many years. Once discovered, concrete pipes large enough for a diver to swim through were added to take advantage of the rich coral and sponge growth. Lots of grouper and cobia on this wreck, and at night sportfishing boats like to try for the mutton snapper and cobia.

Night dives on the wrecks is normally every Saturday night, though the schedule may be expanded to week nights in summer. Boats leave the dock around 6 and anchor over their site just as the sun is setting, twilight dive, while there is still some natural light shining through the water. By the time you surface, the sun is well set. The boats then move shallower to another wreck or to a reef.

Best night dives are on the older, deeper wrecks containing the most coral growth, such as the "Orion" and "Blue Freeze." After sunset, all the coral polyps on both ships make the wrecks appear like a garden in bloom.

Mostkoff says in the future it will be necessary for DERM to rely more heavily on prefabricated items instead of wrecks of opportunity. DERM plans to go out and build a reef by particular design.

Palm Beach and Broward Counties offer a mini-Keys environment much more convenient for weekend trips.

"A planned, designed structure should work better from a fisheries standpoint," Mostkoff explains. "Wrecks offer a limited habitat according to the size of the entrance and exit areas. We've found that certain fish will occupy only very particular areas where these conditions exist.

"We want to design the reefs to control some of the variables by designing a certain size opening and deliberately deploying it in a certain manner," he says.

Mostkoff admits the entire artificial reef program was designed more with the commercial fishing industry in mind than sportfishermen or divers. However, the artificial reefs have become the focal point for all these groups since the natural reef sources are finite and delicate.

When it comes right down to it, the whole concept is to establish new territories as a fisheries resource. That is to everyone's benefit.

The following is a brief list of Miami's artificial reefs as of March, 1992. The information is courtesy of Ben Mostkoff and DERM. For the latest information or to make a donation to DERM's artificial reef fund, call 305/375-DERM.

MATERIAL	DATE SUNK	WATER DEPTH	PROFILE	LORAN-C
TENNECO REEF				
3 shallow structures	10/85	90' 105' 110'	40-50'	14246.9 62122.3
2 deep structures	10/85	185' 190'	74' 83'	14247.2 62120.8
"Cruz Del Sur"	12/86	240'	95'	14246.1 62121.0
HAULOVER REEF				
"Andro"	12/85	103'	38'	14237.7 62129.4
"Rossmerry"	10/85	240'	22'	14239.6 62126.1
"West End"	7/73	228'		14232.4,43111.3
"Hopper Barge"	12/71	234'		14229.5,43113.5
"Ostwind"	6/89	275'	14'	14230.7,62132.2
"Liberty Ship"	5/76	372'		14239.4,43104.5
ANCHORAGE REEF				
"African Queen"	12/86	44'	5'	14229.3,62137.7
"Coquina"	6/87	44'	12'	14228.8,62137.4
"Lands End"	8/84	46'	15'	14229.0,62137.4
"Mary Ann"	8/84	46'	15'	14229.0,62137.4
"Miss karline"	6/89	51'	15'	14229.5,62136.6
KEY BISCAYNE REEF				
"Biscayne"	12/74	55'	15'	14218.5,62145.0
"Miracles-Express"	7/87	55'	25'	14218.5,62145.0
"Proteus"	1/85	72'	30'	14218.7,62144.3
"South Seas"	2/83	73'	15'	14218.2,62144.7
"Sheri-Lyn"	6/87	96'	45'	14218.5,62144.5
"Lakeland"	6/82	126'-140	30'	14218.6,62143,8
RJ DIVING VENTURES REEF				
"Tarpoon"	5/88	71'	29'	14210.2,62151.4
"Moby One"	7/83	97'	10'	14210.2,62151.1
"Hopper Barge"	6/81	163'	40'	14210.3,62149.9

7

TREASURE COAST
FISHING BONANZA

Larry believes the Atlantic's "sailfish alley" is still overlooked.

Sailfish anglers on the "Treasure Coast" wait for cold weather now. That's when the sailfish action is most apt to be reminiscent of the good old days. Although boats won't catch 70 or 80 sails these days, they may catch 20, or even 30 on an exceptional day. In fact, it's still not unusual during a good winter "season" to have four lines hit at the same time by four sails!

A couple of years ago, the seas off Stuart were quite calm for two weeks. The baitfish were abundant during that period and a large congregation of sailfish took up temporary residence in the area. It looked like a "parking lot" out there. Everywhere you looked, according to those who participated, you could see boats hooked up and fighting jumping fish.

Today's boats getting in on the great action in the Atlantic between the Fort Pierce and Jupiter Inlets are usually very conservation minded, according to the locals. While the productivity of those sailfish grounds vary from year to year, most boats will fight a sailfish, then revive and release it. How many they release depends on the cold weather.

"It's the cold snaps up north that bring the sailfish to our shores," an old salt told me. "One year the action is slow, and the next, the fishing is fantastic, perhaps the best in 10 years. You never know."

Fort Pierce/Jupiter

The history of fishing in this region of Florida goes back almost half a century when the small town of Port Salerno was founded as a commercial fishery in the 1940's. Since development is strictly regulated to avoid some of the overpopulation problems that have occurred a few miles south along the Gold Coast, the area remains a relatively quiet fishing community and, incidentally, the home of many boat manufacturers.

This is, in fact, the home of the Whitakers, who helped pioneer sport fishing in the late 20's. Pappy Whitaker was the first to fasten a barber chair in his boat and to position a set of long poles to each side of the boat. That was the beginning of the fighting chair and the outrigger. The improved drop back and spreading apart of the baits would give the fish a chance to get the baits in their mouth.

The Whitaker Boats are still manufactured in Stuart today, and for a trip down memory lane, they have all the old rods and reels that they used back in the early days. They also have plenty of pictures from that past era. Although the items are not readily accessible to public tours, they are often shown to those with a real interest.

Timing The Sails

The sailfish action off Stuart and Jupiter starts generally about the time of the Stuart Light Tackle Tournament in December, and the season runs through February, according to Norm Liebert, manager of the Pirate's Cove Marina. While sails can be caught all year long at the acclaimed "sailfish capital of the world," they're generally around in larger numbers during the three winter months.

It's the predominant northeasterly winds of the first cold fronts that signal the beginning of great fishing. They seem to really pile the sailfish into the area. And, the sailfish may know too when it's best to bite: when the angler has to have one hand on the rod and the other hanging on to the gunwale for safety. Most of the sails run 35 to 40 pounds, but some real monsters have been taken that strained tackle to the limit.

The sails apparently like to stay at the edge of the continental shelf extending between the Palm Beach and Fort Pierce Inlets to spawn. That's one reason why that area is often called "Sailfish

The dolphin action off Stuart and Jupiter is particularly hot in the summer months.

Alley". Like most fish species, they prefer to spawn in the shallow water and feed in the nearby blue water.

Sailfish as little as 8 inches long have been discovered in the offshore grass, and small sails have even been caught in cast nets right off the sea buoy in the Stuart inlet. Another unusual occurrence noted many times by small boats anchored off the beach while fishing for Spanish mackerel is having tiny sailfish chase their spoons!

During most of the warmer months, the predominant winds off the coast between West Palm and Fort Pierce are out of the southeast. They can easily box the compass during a 12 hour period, though, and that can affect fishing in the Stuart area. Further south, in the Palm Beach area, most of the charters have the luxury of fishing semi-protected, deep waters just a mile offshore. The continental shelf is a lot closer to the coast there.

Charter boats out of the Stuart or St. Lucie Inlets must travel at least six miles offshore to start sportfishing. At six miles, the depth is still only 65 feet, but 12 miles out the bottom drops substantially to several hundred fathoms, and that's where the larger bluewater fish, such as marlin and yellowfin tuna, can be caught.

Where To Look

● Most of the charter boats out of Port Salerno start fishing at the Six-mile Reef, a little to the south of the Stuart Inlet. As the current moves boats northward, the most productive captains fish the reef at points where the water color changes, which normally fluctuates with the tide.

There are often some extensive sargasso weed lines in 60 foot of water over the Six-mile Reef which attracts fish from the beginning of the food chain upward. The broad reef there causes tide and current rips and color changes on out to the Eight-mile Reef in 140-foot of water.

● Eight miles offshore, locals normally rig for bluewater fish. One of the most popular sites, "Pushbutton Hill," is located about 12 miles offshore. It's so named because most reef-fishing charter captains use electric reels to haul up some large bottom fish to put meat on the table.

Several productive artificial reefs offshore are placed apart approximately every three or four miles. The locations, marked on most charts, range from 50 feet deep to over 100 feet. Most are sunken ships that lie in areas easily accessible to small boaters.

● One of the ships sunk as part of the area's artificial reef program is the "Liberty Reef" which is just three miles offshore, according to Don Diehl, captain of the "Lady Karin." The 50-foot tall submerged barge sits in 80 feet of water and attracts plentiful grouper and snapper. But you must get them into the boat quickly. Barracuda and shark are always on the lookout for an easy meal there.

Most of the charter boats out of Port Salerno fish the productive Six-mile Reef.

Jacks to 45 pounds, kingfish and cobia also make the area a popular dive spot. There are two extremely strong runs of kingfish each year: February/March and September/October. An additional summer time run occurs near shore. In the summer time, live bait is often used almost within throwing distance of the jetties for the kingfish and cobia. Local captains use greenies or threadfin herring primarily and catch them on gold hooks right outside the Stuart inlet. Live mullet caught by cast netters inshore are also employed.

● A kingfish hole is located to the south of the Stuart Inlet inside the beach reef. At one time, it was actually a natural inlet for the area running from 40 foot of water right into the beach. King mackerel up to 60 pounds are taken there quite often during the summer runs. During cooler weather on any offshore (westerly) wind, the normal size caught is around 30 pounds.

● "Smoker" kings are also taken, along with a variety of bottom fish, off the Golf Ball Water Tower east of Juno Beach. The rugged reef lies in 90 to 220 feet of water. The winter months are almost always good when after king mackerel.

Offshore breezes sometimes dictate green waters with clarity ranging to 30 feet; further offshore the color will change to blue water with underwater visibility up to 100 feet. There is usually good water color somewhere in the area, though, and the charter fleet is pretty adept at finding it.

Offshore Fishing Options

Most of the captains in the Stuart area will ask in advance what type of fishing their clients prefer so that the gear and rigging are appropriate. Charter captains use the artificial reefs to check out the sailfish action, but much of their clientele enjoys angling from an anchored position for amberjack, African pompano, large tiger sharks or an occasional 400-pound Warsaw grouper. Most boats are equipped to fish a variety of ways and handle what bites.

Some captains are better rigged for deep bottom fishing than others without the electric reels. At a cost of about $1,200 for an electric, not all boats can afford them. Consequently, most bottom fishing is done with conventional tackle. But, it is not always easy to hand crank a large fish from several hundred feet down.

Wahoo, which average 30 to 35 pounds off Stuart, are often caught trolling a deep line. Most captains use a planer to take a large Hawaiian Eye and ballyhoo down 30 to 40 feet. Live bait is also used, drifted about 225 feet out. One of the largest wahoo in recent years weighed at the Pirate's Cove Marina reached 103 pounds.

Dolphin up to 60 or 70 pounds have been caught in the area, and, in fact, the 30-pound test record is held by a boat out of Fort Pierce with a 70-pound fish. They can be caught year around and are the mainstay of fishing during the summer. People more often than not take the delicacy home and eat it. Night fishing for swordfish is another summer option.

For sport, try a shark trip, offered by many charters. At certain times of year, hammerheads are so thick that as soon as a live bait enters the water, sharks will appear. Every year over labor day weekend, a shark tournament is held off Stuart. It's a three-day marathon, including all night. Just have the fish weighed in by Sunday.

```
┌─────────────────────────────────────────────────────────────────┐
│                  Calendar - South Atlantic Coast                  │
│                                                                   │
│   SPRING          SUMMER             FALL              WINTER     │
│   Sailfish        Sailfish           Sailfish          Sailfish   │
│   Pompano         Dolphin            Drum              Drum       │
│   Bluefish        King Mackerel      Flounder          Flounder   │
│   Sea Trout       Bonito             Sea Trout         Bluefish   │
│   Sheepshead      Spanish Mackerel   Spanish Mackerel  Redfish    │
│   Grouper         Amberjack          Grouper           Sea Trout  │
│   Snapper         Bluefish           Snapper           Grouper    │
│                   Tarpon             Redfish           Snapper    │
│                   Grouper            King Mackerel                │
│                   Snapper                                         │
│                   Flounder                                        │
└─────────────────────────────────────────────────────────────────┘
```

"You can get skunked offshore any time of the year, but you can also catch just about anything at any time of the year," says Capt. Liebert. "Dolphin, sailfish, wahoo, kingfish, bonito, barracuda and most other sportfish can be found pretty much year round. Marlin start showing up in March and run through April. At other times, the fishing may be a mixture; some fish are leaving and others are coming in."

Inshore Fishing Options

If the ocean isn't too stirred up, the St. Lucie Inlet running into the Indian River, will be fairly clear, leaving some inshore options available for the light tackle angler. There are usually plenty of ocean snook, sea trout, channel bass, redfish and pompano for inshore fishermen. Sheepshead, drum, croakers and ladyfish are also taken.

The St. Lucie River is also very popular with snook fisherman. The fish which can get up to 40 pounds, are often caught on live bait like mullet, pilchard, etc. It's a rather inexpensive means of fishing if you wade the river while the snook are running.

"We've caught snook weighing 25 pounds right off the dock, "says Liebert. "A gold spoon can be very effective."

65

Bluefish are a challenging quarry off the Treasure Coast.

"The Cross Florida Canal gives us quite an influx of fresh water into the river system here," he adds. "At one time, the water at Pirate's Cove was crystal clear. That was back in the '40's. But when the Corps opened the canal, it killed all the oyster beds and clam beds. I guess that's progress!"

Regardless, there are still a lot of productive areas accessible to small boaters. Bluefish and Spanish mackerel are found in the

There are a lot of productive areas accessible to small boaters.

sheltered waters. The jetties are inaccessible from land, but do provide excellent fishing structure. In winter time, though, the wave action around the jetties and inlets may just be too much for most small boats.

You'll find some bottom fishing action in the river during the winter when the winds are really blowing. In fact, it is not unusual to see charter parties fishing those inshore waters then. A 46-footer troller fishing for bluefish in the river may look funny to some, but at times, it has to be done.

On the other hand, the seas in the summer may be so calm that you can practically chase dolphin in a john boat! It's like that in the Atlantic off Stuart; the fish are usually there waiting.

Convenient Accommodations and Access

One of the most convenient accommodations to charters in the Port St. Lucie/Stuart area is the all-inclusive Club Med Sandpiper. Totally renovated and with a truly French flair, it is the only Club Med facility to offer daily rates. This is a particularly attractive place for families and anglers. Fishing charters for up to five people are easily arranged through the Guest Services office. Half-day charters are available which include transportation to and from the marina and lunch. Full day charters are also available. The best rates are September through November. For current costs contact any travel agent or Club Med toll free at 1-800-CLUB-MED.

Another great base of operation is the Indian River Plantation Resort and Marina on Hutchinson Island off Stuart. It has a 77-slip full-service marina with deep-sea and river fishing charters. The 200-acre property has various summer and fall packages that the avid angler may enjoy. For information, contact the resort at 1-407-225-3700 or write them at 555 N.E. Ocean Blvd., Hutchinson Island, Stuart, FL 34996.

Port St. Lucie, Fort Pierce and Stuart are all extremely accessible by air, land or sea. Boaters can cruise the Intracoastal Waterway to reach Fort Pierce; Port St. Lucie and Stuart are just around the bend from Sewalls Point in the St. Lucie River Inlet.

The man-made inlet is used by many area marinas to exit to blue waters, however, it can be treacherous in the winter with a northeasterly blowing. A sandbar at the mouth of the inlet can also cause problems to boaters unfamiliar with the waters when the sea is running or during an outgoing tide.

The nearest commercial airports are at Fort Pierce and West Palm Beach, which are served daily by most major airlines connecting to these cities through Orlando or Miami. Road travelers can use the Florida Turnpike or I-95 to reach the Fort Pierce exit and travel south on U.S. 1 to Port St. Lucie or Stuart. For a free Florida map write the Florida Division of Tourism or any of the area chambers of commerce.

Free concrete ramps and parking space are available at the Chamber of Commerce in Shephard Park downtown just off U.S. Hwy 1; in Sandsprit Park southeast of Stuart near Port Salerno; and at Casa Rio Boat Basin in Rio. Other natural launching sites are located at the Indian River Causeway, the Stuart and Jensen Beach bridges and north of Stuart into the St. Lucie River.

8

OCEAN FLOOR LUXURIES

Tim reveals the Gold Coast's best glitter is on the many wrecks deliberately sunk to attract divers and fish.

The Florida Keys may be the most-dived spot in the entire world, but another part of South Florida is fighting hard to short-stop traveling divers by luring them to their own wrecks and reefs.

They are Palm Beach and Broward Counties, the famed Gold Coast that boasts mile after mile of ultra-posh million-dollar real estate. Their diver enticement programs are working so well they've quickly become Florida's second most popular dive destination.

And it hasn't hurt that nature is on their side. Except for the Keys, the one place where the warm waters of the Gulf Stream come closest to land is off Palm Beach. As Gold Coast dive promoters like to point out, you'll find many of the same warm water conditions and species as in the Keys, so why go the extra distance?

Especially when the locals are this serious: the Palm Beach County Artificial Reef Committee sank a mint condition Rolls Royce Silver Cloud in 1985 as its first diver-attractor. That is a heck of a statement.

However, Broward County and Fort Lauderdale are perhaps even more intent on enticing divers. They upped Palm Beach one

69

better by towing the "Mercedes I," a 200-foot freighter grounded on the deck of a Palm Beach swimming pool, and dropping it on the bottom a mile off Fort Lauderdale.

No other area outside the Keys has sought divers as earnestly as these two Gold Coast counties. As more people explored the area, Floridians discovered they had a mini-Keys environment in a far more northerly location, an area much more convenient for weekend trips. The Keys are terrific--no one ever contradicts that--but the long drive can be too far for short one and two-day bounce dives.

As word of the new gold strike spread among Floridians, dive operations began to proliferate and prosper, to the extent that today the Gold Coast ranks as Florida's No. 2 dive destination. Despite their increased popularity, Gold Coast dive sites are never as crowded as the Pennekamp area. In addition, the sites tend to be so spread out with such a variety to choose from, you don't find yourself crowded elbow to flipper like spiny lobsters on a migration march. Plus, many of the sites are only 20 minutes or so from shore. At the city of Delray, you can even wreck dive by swimming right from the beach, just as in the Caribbean.

The profuse marine life includes plenty of deep water inhabitants not normally encountered in so close to shore. The reason is the Gulf Stream, the warm water current that brings in such creatures as ocean sunfish, logger head turtles, sharks, big rays and other pelagic species.

But the Gulf Stream--which some divers refer to as the underwater version of the jet stream--also creates a substantial current through the deeper sites. Divers don't attempt to battle this 3-4 knot force but join it instead, using a style of diving that enables them to drift with the current, to go with the flow rather than against it. Gold Coast divers cover considerable territory without wearing themselves out.

Palm Beach County

The shallow reefs (20-30 feet) off Palm Beach are mainly clusters or patches, but those in deep water are true reefs, part of the continuous line that begins at Boca Raton and extends northward to Jupiter.

The 200-foot freighter, Mercedes, sunk off Fort Lauderdale in 1985, is now overgrown with coral, heavily populated with fish and is one of the most popular dive sites in the southern Atlantic. (photo by Don Rogers, courtesy of Ft. Lauderdale Convention & Visitors Bureau).

71

The most popular of these is called the Double Ledges, in 75 to 85 feet of water. The current can vary considerably from one day to the next, but it's always best to come expecting the strongest. That way, you'll be pleasantly surprised if it's not. However, as the reef runs north-south and the Gulf Stream flows northward, this is a perfect arrangement for drift diving. As the Double Ledges are quite close to the Gulf Stream, the marine life can be outstanding, depending on whether a turtle, ray or shark is passing through. The angelfish found on this reef are among the largest seen anywhere, including the Keys.

Drift diving is a favorite way of moving through the area, letting the current of the nearby Gulf Stream provide all the action while you simply float over the coral heads. This can be an exciting, wild ride which permits you to see much more that you could normally view by swimming. Also, since little exertion is required, your air tends to last longer so you can stay longer. Drift diving does require special advance planning since there isn't any way to return to your boat if it's been anchored. Your dive boat needs to drift along with you, following your air bubbles, so that when you do ascend it's standing by ready to take you back aboard. Unless you have a friend willing to sit out the diving, you'll need to take turns, each buddy-pair taking its turn while the other is operating the boat.

Closer to shore and usually not as affected by current is the popular Breakers Reef, located in front of the famous Breakers Hotel. Because of its mild current, this is a favorite spot for newcomers. The Breakers Reef offers most of the things divers hope to see--snapper, lobster, tropical fish, morays and turtles--and it doesn't require the skill or effort needed farther offshore. The Breakers Reef plunges as much as 75 feet on the outer edge. This can be an especially good site for viewing or photographing the swarms of small fish. Barracuda are also present in force, though they never present a problem.

You'll find shallower reef spots in the same vicinity, including the Cable Crossing -- a favorite for check-out dives because it rarely has much current, and the tropical fish, sponges and corals there are a good introduction for first-time ocean divers

As for wrecks, the "Mispah" is one of the best known in the country. Like many of the region's more modern wrecks, it was deliberately sunk to serve as a fish attractor. It has performed remarkably well and now houses some of the largest angel fish I've ever seen. The "Mispah," however, wasn't placed at the bottom to provide a convenient hunting ground for spearfishermen. As a matter of fact, the wreck is a protected site and spearguns are not allowed. Therefore the fish life can be excellent, some days rivaling what you can see in the Keys.

If you go inside the frame of the ship, you can often duck the current, letting it flow around and over you. Putting yourself into one of the ship's protective openings and into comparatively calmer water is like slamming the door on a windstorm.

The "Mispah" is covered with corals, sponges and hydroids. Its deck is strewn with wreckage and the sides breached in several places. The ship seems to be a relic of war. This, combined with the depth and dark blue water, sometimes results in a very eerie dive. My most memorable dive here was the time a large ray swam over us. Busy with my photography, it had not occurred to me to look up, and it was my buddy who first sighted the creature.

It moved over us in a slow, majestic manner. Spotting our air bubbles, it made a kind of banking turn as if to look at us. We must have startled it, for a moment later its wings began flapping very fast. It swam swiftly and erratically, the flapping wings a blurred illusion: like a wind-up toy gone out of control. That was one of the most amusing sights I've ever seen underwater.

About 300 yards from the "Mispah" is the wreck of the "Amarilys," a 44-foot steel freighter in open sand. Only the hull and deck remain.

Also not far from the "Mispah" is "Spearman's Barge," typical of the many barges found up and down the coast. Because of the prolific marine life that's taken up residence, it is an excellent photography site. Just how good was several years ago when "Popular Photography" published my article on underwater macro photography. I sent the editor slides I'd taken all over the world, but two of the six selected for publication were shot on that barge. Since then, I've come to appreciate the barge even more.

In some spots the sponge growth is so thick that fish burrow inside it like rabbits. Obscured among the corals and sponges is the unusual thorny oyster--a mollusk whose top shell has a brittle streamer resembling a scooped and clipped piece of salt water taffy.

A mile southeast of the Palm Beach Inlet is Artificial Reef Site 2, begun in 1985 and the real declaration of war between Palm Beach and Broward Counties to prove who had the biggest and the most. Artificial Reef Site 2, with depths varying from 80 to 90 feet, consists of three different objects.

Largest is the "Owens," a 125-foot freighter resting upright less than 10 minutes from the inlet. You can enter the cargo holds and crew's quarters and exit through holes blown in the hull to sink the ship. From its second day, a resident school of barracuda has stayed to patrol the wreck. Grouper are also regular residents.

Look off the bow, and you can see underwater the two other pieces of reef, a Rolls Royce and a barge. The Rolls, also sunk in 1985, was quite a sight when it first went down. Regrettably, it was quickly stripped of its hood ornament and everything else not bolted down. Look for lobster in the back seat and school fish under the hood. The barge wreck normally has grouper and nurse sharks nestled under its prow, with snapper much more obvious around the bow.

Because of the direction of flow, you can drift all three spots on one dive if you start at the barge, then drift to the car and the "Owens."

Down in the town of Delray, 150 yards from the south end of the public beach, is the "Delray Wreck," a pretzled mass of steel hull freighter sunk in the 1920s. Lots of corals and tropicals and the bottom is only 22 feet. However, boat traffic is heavy on weekends. And if you dive from the beach, don't forget to tote a float flying the dive flag.

Local dive shops or the tourist board can tell you of other popular sites all just a little more than swimming distance from the Palm Beach Inlet.

Broward County

Two other popular resort areas, Pompano Beach and Fort Lauderdale, also have inlets that allow dive boats easy access to their respective locations, though there may be some overlap as the two are so close together. Divers don't mind: that gives them a sampling of both areas.

Pompano Beach reefs are characterized by ledges that rise 10-15 feet above the sand shelf. Like those off the Palm Beaches, they are littered with colorful sponges filled with many small invertebrates. Lobstering can be quite good, particularly at night when the crustaceans are more likely to walk the reefs openly. Wrecks, too, are interesting, including several that date back to the 1700s.

To get an idea just how good the diving around Fort Lauderdale is, consider that the reefs running south between Port Everglades Inlet to Dania are being considered as the location for Florida's second underwater park. When/if created, this means the reefs would be completely protected like those at Pennekamp, exempt from spearing, fish traps, tropical fish collecting, dredging, or removal of any artifacts deemed of historic interest. Boats will be allowed to anchor only at specific moorings or in the sand. The reef section would be a giant look-but-don't-touch playground.

Rare pillar corals, staghorn, star and brain corals are all to be found in the proposed park section at Cuda Reef and Hammer Head Reef. Many divers feel the protection can't come too soon; some corals are showing some damaged from dredging and pollution.

Wreck divers have some unusual options to choose from: a houseboat, several barges, and a tug boat in addition to the 435-foot Lowrance Artificial Reef, sunk in 200 feet of water in 1984 and reputed to be the largest ship sunk intact for an artificial reef anywhere on the U.S. Eastern Seaboard.

The diving from Hollywood to Lauderdale is characterized by three sets of reef lines which lie progressively farther offshore. The first line is only about 300 yards from the beach and is in fairly shallow water, less than 25 feet in most places. You can usually find lots of tropicals, swimming over the reef, and some lobster. Since this reef line is fairly close to land, it can be reached by swimming but you definitely need a diver's flag to warn the boats away; further, state law also requires it.

The second reef line varies from one-half to three quarters of a mile out, with depths averaging around 30 feet. You'll find about the same marine life here as at the first one. The third reef line is probably the best. It is located about a mile out in deeper water. This is where you'll normally find the larger fish and coral life--and also a lot of boat traffic on weekends. This third reef is the best place for the more experienced diver interested in photography and collecting.

It's no secret that in recent years severe storm fronts have severely damaged reefs throughout many parts of the Gold Coast. Pollution and fresh water discharge from the Intracoastal Waterway have also taken their toll.

But the situation is not as bad as it might seem. Broward County keeps adding new underwater attractions, ships deliberately sunk as artificial reefs to attract marine life. More than two dozen derelict freighters and other vessels are sunk off Broward County, primarily around Fort Lauderdale and Pompano.

Besides developing some impressive sponge and coral growth in a fairly short period of time, these shipwrecks now transformed into "shipreefs" are proven fish attractors. Sergeant majors, sea turtles, octopus, butterfly fish, barracudas--even sailfish and tuna--are sighted around them with regularity.

Artificial reef building has been underway since 1968, but gained momentum after 1981 when the Environmental Protection District assumed leadership. Fort Lauderdale has been pursuing its reef building program so aggressively it literally took away from Palm Beach the most publicized derelict vessel of the last half of the 20th century. It was the "Mercedes I," which received worldwide TV coverage when the German freighter grounded itself on Thanksgiving Day, 1984, in the backyard swimming pool of Palm Beach socialite Mollie Wilmot.

● Following a cleanup to remove potential pollutants and physical hazards, the 198-foot "Mercedes I" was towed south to within a mile of Fort Lauderdale and sent to the bottom with a series of strategically placed explosions. Unlike some other highly publicized reefs-in the making where the sinking hulks sometimes flip or drift in the wrong direction, the "Mercedes I" came to rest upright in 98 feet of water.

● In 1985, the Houston-based Tenneco Oil Co. donated two drilling platforms and the deck of a third which were placed at the south end of the Broward County line. A vast improvement over the old tire dumping routine--125,000 tires in the late 70s for artificial reefs which turned out to be lousy.

● The Tenneco Towers, one of the largest artificial reefs off South Florida, are a mile off Hallandale Beach. All 3 sections line up with the water tower standing in front of the radio antenna. They are well covered with octocorals and hard corals are taking a firm grip. Jacks, Spanish hogfish, queen angels and schools of baitfish swarm the towers. Two decked sections, situated in 110 feet of water, rise to within 60 feet of the surface with a 20-foot span between them. There's a shallower, smaller platform. The supporting legs are resting on a bottom too deep for sport divers: 190 feet. (LORAN: 14246.9 62122.7)

● In 1991, the 240-foot long "Poinciana" joined the ghost fleet as did a 114-foot freighter in just 71 feet of water.

Dive operators have a choice of 80 different sites on the 23-mile long, 1-1/2 to 2-mile wide Fort Lauderdale Reef. Average visibility is 40 to 60 feet and water temperatures dip to the high 60s or low 70s in winter, definitely full wet suit conditions. Calmest weather (and when visibility may reach 60 to 100 feet) is from the end of May until October. Winter winds make dive pretty much of a crap shoot; it all depends on whether a front is churning up the ocean.

Ask about the special dive packages that are almost as popular in Broward County as they are in the Caribbean. You can arrange special dive packages including double accommodations and 2-tank dive boat trip for about the regular hotel price. Many specials are 3-days, 2-nights and usually include breakfast; add-on days at special rates are also available.

Prices are cheapest in summer, when diving conditions are at their best. Rather than gamble winter vacation time here, go to the Caribbean where weather is more of a sure thing. Remember, the coastal diving conditions are "iffy" anywhere in Florida from October through May.

Broward County Artificial Reef Program

● ANCIENT MARINER Depth 70' Loran C: 14281.0, 62088.6 After sinking at its berth and being the site of the largest hepatitis outbreak in Florida's history, the Ancient Mariner was finally sunk as an artificial reef on June 9, 1991. Three other vessels are located nearby including the Berry Patch.

● BERRY PATCH Depth: 65' Loran C: 14281.1, 62088.5. The Berry Patch, a 65' steel tug, was built in 1940 and was sunk on Aug 15, 1987. Also at this location is a 40' steel boat hull and a 50' steel houseboat which lies 100' to the SW. The Ancient Mariner lies to the NW.

● BILL BOYD REEF Depth: 265' Loran C: 14265.8, 62102.4. This 211' German freighter was sunk on July 18, 1986 and was renamed in honor of a "pioneer" in sportfishing. A world record mutton snapper was caught at this location in May of 1988.

● BUDDY MERRITT REEF Depth: 414' Loran C: 14275.6, 62089.9 This 70' steel barge with a welded superstructure constructed of heavy yacht cradles was sunk on Dec 17, 1987 and is located in Rodeo Reef Site. This is a favorite deepwater spot of charter skippers.

● BUD KROHN REEF Depth: 440' Loran C: 14269.8, 62095.4. This deepwater reef consists of a 183' Spanish-built freighter. Sunk on Dec 3, 1989, it's located offshore of Galt Ocean Mile directly between the two inlets. Funds for this project were raised in part by the South Florida Fishing Classic.

● CAICOS EXPRESS Depth 237' Loran C: 14271.8, 62096.2, a 188' Dutch freighter, was sunk on Nov 12, 1985.

● CAPT DAN Depth: 110' Loran C: 14272.3, 62096.9. This 175' ex Coast Guard buoy tender (Hollyhock WLM 220) was sunk on Feb 20, 1990 in memory of Capt Dan Garnsey. The funds to purchase the vessel came from the Florida Boating Improvement Program.

● COREY N'CHRIS' REEF Depth: 244' Loran C: 14274.4, 62093.4. A 130' dredge was sunk off Pompano Pier on May 18, 1986 in conjunction with the Pompano Beach Fishing Rodeo.

● CRUZ DEL SUR Depth: 230' Loran C: 14246.2, 62121.1. A 257' German freighter was sunk as a joint project with Metro Dade County on Dec 19, 1986. This reef is located south of the Tenneco Towers and north of Haulover Inlet.

● DANIA PIER EROJACKS Depth: 10-20' Loran C: 14253.2, 62121.1. Thousands of concrete erojacks extend several hundred feet in an east-west direction. The erojacks, built as an unsuccessful erosion control device, form an excellent artificial reef.

● RODEO DIVERS REEF (qualmann Tugs) Depth: 78' Loran C: 14273.6, 62096.0. This reef consists of two tugboats and several smaller boats.

● TE AMO REEF Depth: 190' Loran C: 14261.8, 62106.6. The 100' wooden racing ketch was sunk May 16, 1985. It was once owned by the author Somerset Maugham.

● TENNECO DEEP REEF Depth: 105' Loran C: 14246.9, 62122.7. Located directly west of TENNECO DEEP REEF, this reef consists of three oil production decks. Both Tenneco Reefs line up with the Hallandale water tower directly in front of the "basket tower" radio antenna. The smaller (western) deck section is reported to have collapsed.

● TRACOR DRYDOCK REEF (Nova Deepwater Reef) Depth: 220' Loran C: 14261.2, 62107.4. A 200' US Navy Floating Drydock, AFDL-8, was sunk June 22, 1982. Also at this location are Chris Craft hull molds placed by Bahia Mar charter skippers, Captains Harold Barnhardt, Bill Robinson, Harold Vreeland, and Jack Wittenborn, considered the fathers of the current artificial reef program.

● REBEL REEF Depth 110' Loran C: 14267.1, 62130.0. Sunk July 16, 1985, this 150' Norwegian coastal freighter lies pointing north near the outside edge of the third reef. Purchased at Federal Auction by a Fort Lauderdale attorney and environmentalist who donated the vessel to Broward County.

● RENEGADE REEF Depth: 190' Loran C: 14273.4, 62094.6. A 150' Dutch coastal freighter, sunk July 10, 1985, is located a few hundred yards north of the Lowrance at the Rodeo Reef Site. The Renegade was donated by the anglers fishing on the fishing boat "Renegade" with the winning prize money from the 1985 Pompano Beach Fishing Rodeo.

● RIVER BEND REEF Depth: 98' Loran C: 14263.9, 62106.4. Numerous wood vessels, all in 30-50' range in size, are located north of the Houseboat. These vessels were donated and placed by River Bend Marine.

● ROBERT EDMISTER REEF Depth: 70' Loran C: 14264.7, 62106.7. This former 95' Coast Guard Cutter was sunk on December 11, 1989, approximately 1,500 feet due south of the "Jay Scutti."

● RODEO 25 Depth: 122' Loran C: 14273.8, 62095.3. On May 12, 1990, in front of approximately 100,000 spectators, a 215' freighter was sunk to celebrate the Pompano Beach Fishing Rodeo's 25th anniversary. This is one of the few wrecks off Broward's coast that lies in an east/west direction.

● RONALD B. JOHNSON REEF Depth: 230' Loran C: 14274.3, 62093.3. On May 15, 1988, the Ronald B. Johnson was sunk offshore of the Pompano Pier. This 230' freighter is dedicated to America's Vietnam veterans and is located at the Rodeo Reef Site.

● MILLER LITE Depth: 155' Loran C: 14274.5, 62094.1. This 186' refrigerated cargo ship, built in 1957, was sunk May 17, 1987 and is part of the Rodeo Reef.

● NOULA EXPRESS Depth: 71' Loran C: 14283.3, 62085.4. This 114' Danish freighter, built in 1939, was sunk on July 12, 1988 in a joint project with Palm Beach County. Now lying on the Broward/Palm Beach County line, the ship is one of the most popular diving wrecks in South Florida.

● OSBORNE REEF Depth: 60-65' Loran C: 14263.3, 62107.9. A 60' barge scattered tires, fuel tanks, 300 tons of concrete culvert, and a circle of erojacks were placed in the 1970's as part of the BAR, Inc Reef Program.

● PAPA'S REEF Depth: 270' Loran C: 14274.8, 62092.6. The 170' freighter, built in Holland in 1955, was sunk on May 14, 1989 in conjunction with the Pompano Beach Fishing Rodeo. This deepwater wreck has become the home to many large gamefish and conservation is especially important when fishing on these artificial reefs.

● PORT EVERGLADES REEF Depth: 140-150' Loran C: 14261.9, 62107.5. Eight barge loads of 50 ton concrete blocks and concrete piles deployed in Jan of 1989 have become a very productive site for various species of snapper..

● JAY SCUTTI REEF Depth: 67' Loran C: 14265.2, 62106.3. This former Aruba harbor tug was sunk on Sept 19, 1986. The Dutch built tug is one of Florida's most popular wreck dives.

● JIM ATRIA REEF Depth: 112' Loran C: 14266.5, 62103.5. This 1961 Dutch-built freighter, sunk Sept 23, 1987, is lying on its port side and is pointing North, therefore, extra caution must be exercised to avoid being disoriented.

● KORNAHRENS REEF Depth 135' and 359' Loran C: (Shallow) 14272.4, 62097.0 (Deep) 14273.1, 62094.0. In December of 1990, 1800 tons of anti-submarine netting were transported and donated by Rob Kornahrens, a Pompano businessman. These heavy steel nets protected Guantanamo Bay, Cuba from German subs during WWII. They were stored on Hospital Cay, Cuba until deployed at two sites offshore of Pompano Beach.

● LOWRANCE REEF Depth: 190-210' Loran C: 14273.0, 62095.3. This 435' Canadian built freighter, the largest artificial reef on the Atlantic Coast, was sunk March 31, 1984. This was the first vessel sunk in the Rodeo Reef site. The ship was stranded in Port Everglades for a number of years prior to being deployed as a reef.

● MARRIOTT REEF Depth: 70' Loran C: 14261.4, 62109.8. A 1945 C-54 airplane sunk Nov 23, 1985 is the most famous artificial reef in the world. The Mercedes washed up on socialite Mollie Wilmot's Palm Beach estate during the Thanksgiving Day storm of 1984. The cost of the purchase of the vessel came from the Florida Boating Improvement Program (boat registration fees). The clean-up of the vessel was donated by South Florida Divers SCUBA club.

9

ISLAND SNOOK &
OTHER FARE

The Lower Gulf Coast offers Larry's favorite "laid-back" inshore fishing

The area along the backside of Cayo Costa is swept by the tide, and that's where guide Larry Mendez, Bill Cork of Plano, Illinois, and I were drifting our sardines. The six-inch long baitfish were frisky and that kind of action attracts fish, plenty of them.

We had boated four large trout when a large snook finally ate my "white bait" and made off through the grassy depths toward the pass. I worked the fish from the shallow beach area to the deeper water near the boat. After performing four aerial maneuvers, an exhausted 14 pounder pointed its mouth in my direction and spit out the hook. It slowly swam toward the bottom to rest and regain strength.

While we didn't get to photograph the catch, I had my thrill and was happy. Mendez maintained our position on that particular hole with an anchor, and it wasn't long before Cork had a 12 pound snook. He brought his next to the boat before it, too, broke the line and swam away. Our luck, at least, was consistent. We had a couple more snook on that day, but to be honest, 15 trout and a like number of redfish kept interrupting the snook action.

It's like that in Pine Island Sound, just south of Charlotte Harbor in Southwest Florida. On some days, all you can catch are

81

snook, and on others, the redfish and trout action is hot too. In pursuit of snook, anglers on the West Coast of Florida use a variety of techniques. Some days, the snook won't leave a Cotee Jig alone, and on others, they prefer live baitfish.

Anglers catch Pine Island snook on all types of bass lures. Vibrating plugs, like Rat-L-Traps, jerkbaits and crankbaits all have a following, but the jig is probably the best artificial to use in these shallow, weedy waters. The most popular colors are white or red, or a combination of white and red or white and green. When the lure action is slow, then live bait can often catch a snook or two.

Snook are common along the mangrove islands scattered among the thousands of acres of grass flats that line the barrier islands, sounds and bays around Fort Myers. Some of the better snook concentrations can be found around the docks at the edge of the deep grass flats on the north end of Pine Island around Bokeelia Point. Many shore-bound anglers catch huge snook beneath the docks from which they have access.

Another good area to search for snook is near the mangrove treeline and three foot deep flat on the west side of the Sound near a pass adjacent to Cape Haze. The area just off the North Captiva airport runway is a known haven for some giant snook. The docks along that island and the others around the Sound seem to also harbor some monster snook. A friend has taken big snook weighing up to 34 pounds from docks near several of the passes.

Island Passes

The Pine Island Sound area offers a variety of structural habitat such as docks and wood pilings, beaches, grass beds, mangrove islands, plus other influencing factors for a snook fisherman, including incoming and outgoing tides, finger channels, eddies and passes separating the islands of North Captiva, Cayo Costa, Boca Grande, Captiva and Sanibel. Snook can be found any number of places around the grassy rips or markers lining the Intracoastal Waterway.

Another good high-tide area for big snook is around Sanibel Pier. During low tide levels, look for finger channels just off the mangrove islands that offer strong tidal flows. They usually cut through large grass beds and around barrier mangrove islands.

Snook are common along the mangrove islands scattered among the thousands of acres of grass flats that line the barrier islands, sounds and bays around Fort Myers.

When water levels drop due to the outgoing tide, the surrounding grass beds will usually be exposed, pushing the snook within these channels.

Mendez prefers to fish in an area with abundant bait fish present. If the forage is not moving in the proper areas, he'll often "seed" the spot with a handful of baits. When using white bait or shiners, the guide will use a 2/0 hook and 40 pound test leader. The stronger leader is a good choice when heavy snook are in and around

83

pilings or other obstructions. Larger white bait is ideal for bigger snook, and they can carry a slightly heavier leader.

"Speckled" bottom, with sandy potholes surrounded by grass near mangroves, is ideal for snook, according to Mendez. In waters of two or three feet, you can also catch both trout and redfish. Depths of 7 to 8 feet lie adjacent to the better flats. When the falling tide practically dries up the flats, snook will move off into the deeper waters nearby.

Pine Island Sound Trout

Fishing white bait for some of the big trout that show up in the grass flats off Charlotte Harbor each spring and early summer can be exciting. Rick Markesbery joined Mendez and I on one search for big trout. Rick is an avid angler and knows the area well, having fished it for over 10 years.

We started off the day fishing the north end of Pine Island at a place called Bokeelia Point. Two trout, a jack and a large ladyfish gave us some action initially, but then slow times set in. We moved across the Sound to a three foot deep flat near a pass off Cape Haze.

Our sardines were cast into the grassy depths just off the bar. The spot was ideal, and there the trout awaited food and our presentations. The movement of the water coming out of the bay over the grass flat pushed the baitfish off a shallow point right into the deeper water in front of us. Too, as the water on the flat began to drop, the schools of white bait present dropped off into the deeper area. As we sat on that one spot, the three of us caught a dozen trout, most of which were between 16 and 24 inches long.

Speckled trout are very common among the thousand of acres of grass flats that line the barrier islands, sounds and bays along the lower Gulf Coast. In pursuit of the trout, anglers use a variety of techniques to lure this most popular table fare species. While some offer live bait presentations, artificial lures as jigs, Rat-L Traps, spoons, jerk baits and crankbaits are most common. The most popular lure colors are white and red, white and green, white, or red.

To secure enough white bait for a day's outing, there are several conditions with which to contend. Seasons, as well as structure, play an important part. Usually in April through June, the baitfish are located along beaches, grass beds and the passes separating the

Calendar - Southern Gulf Coast

SPRING	SUMMER	FALL	WINTER
Sailfish	Sailfish	Sailfish	Sailfish
Dolphin	Dolphin	Dolphin	Dolphin
Wahoo	Amberjack	Wahoo	Wahoo
Barracuda	Barracuda	Bluefish	Barracuda
Bluefish	Spanish Mackerel	King Mackerel	Sea Trout
King Mackerel	Sea Trout	Sea Trout	Redfish
Pompano	Whiting	Redfish	Bonito
Spanish Mackerel	Pompano	Snook	
Redfish		Spanish Mackerel	
Snook		Whiting	
Sea Trout			
Grouper			
Snapper			

islands from Sanibel Island north to Charlotte Harbor. Other good areas at times include the tripods, grassy rips and markers lining the Intracoastal Waterway.

Favorite areas for most local experts are those which have developed sand shoals. They are normally found between the Intracoastal Waterway and the passes that separate the barrier islands. The most productive sand shoals are shoals that are covered with grass beds that are close to deeper water.

Gathering Spots

A favorite white bait area is called Hell's Half Acre, a huge sandbar located just east of North Captiva Pass. Through the weed-covered sandbar are small cuts and channels that have deeper water coming into the area. What makes it an excellent location is that it's the first location off the Gulf of Mexico coming through the pass; when the baitfish come in, they quickly move into the weedbeds.

When approaching these shoals, do so at slow speed. If the water is fairly calm, keep your eyes open for silver flashes as the baits dimple the surface of the water. Also look for pelicans and other birds diving into the water; pelicans feed on the white bait and can help locate the schools. One method to attract white bait within cast net distance is to use chum, a mixture of one can of mackerel mixed with a loaf of bread and a little water to thin it. Once a few baits are attracted to the chum, masses soon move in.

Chumming for white bait is best when the tide is moving - an oil slick on the surface then will help to attract bait from about 100 feet or so away. While you can catch them on a low tide or dead tide, the best catch normally occurs after the tide has started moving back in. The larger white bait is most available in the spring when the water temperature hits 70 degrees. That seems to be the magic number for finding an abundance of the baitfish.

After mid-June, the larger white bait becomes harder to find in this area. Smaller ones are still fairly numerous, though, and they will work, but the average size trout may be smaller as well. Most of my fishing in the area has centered around the flats and docks off the islands of North Captiva, Cayo Costa and Pine Island Sound. I'll normally focus on shallow weedbeds and on docks.

The trout in Pine Island Sound are always eager for white bait. Another good area for bigger trout is the grass beds off Sanibel Pier. During low tide levels, look also for finger channels that are formed by tidal flows located in the flats. They usually cut through large grass beds and around barrier mangrove islands. An outgoing tide and dropping water levels will expose the surrounding grass beds and push large schools of trout within these channels.

Redfish Harbor

Not all the fish you catch in such places will be trout. On one morning, our five-inch long baits drew a different crowd. Rick's white bait landed on a small sand pothole in the grass and quickly had company. Three reds charged the bait and one was successful in beating his competition. Rick set back on the rod and hooked solid into a redfish. It sprinted across the speckled bottom of grass and sand toward deeper water.

My lure was tossed into the mass of reds, and one charged it as it neared the boat. The strike was jolting and the 20-pound red took off for parts unknown. The drags were singing on my reel and Rick's when Mendez joined the fun with still another red. The triple was

In Southwest Florida, the sandy potholes surrounded by grass in one to three feet are ideal for site fishing the reds. Depths of 7 to 8 feet lie adjacent to the better flats. When the falling tide practically dries up the speckled bottom, the redfish will move off into the deeper waters nearby.

not long lasting, as one threw the hook. Rick's and my red were both fighting a bully battle that saw us snub the fish's runs, gain line and then lose it to the reds as they screamed across the flats.

My line soon accumulated a small mass of weeds about five feet above the red, and I worried that the 8 pound test line might not fare well. I worked the fish to the boat and Mendez helped remove the weeds prior to hoisting it aboard. After a few photos, we placed the fish back into the water and watched it swim away. The stocky fish measured 32 inches, my largest red to date.

Speckled bottom is usually good for both trout and redfish. In Southwest Florida, the sandy potholes surrounded by grass in one to three feet are ideal for site fishing the reds. Depths of 7 to 8 feet lie adjacent to the better flats. When the falling tide practically dries up the speckled bottom, the redfish will move off into the deeper waters nearby.

Other Opportunities

Offshore anglers can find king and Spanish mackerel, and bottom fishermen can catch grouper at a place called the "Ice Box." The area of rocky bottom with numerous ravines is located in 50 feet of water about five miles southwest of Sarasota. Another area west of Sarasota in 30 feet of water offers excellent fishing for the mackerel species plus bluefish in the summer months. Rocky formations attract the fish.

More Information

For further information about fishing in the area, contact the Lee Island Coast Visitor & Convention Bureau. Those fishing the Naples area will be very pleased with the Edgewater Beach Hotel, an all-suite hotel at 1901 Gulf Shore Blvd. North, Naples, FL 33940 or phone 800/821-0196 or 813/262-6511.

For an excellent booklet showing area accommodations ask for the "Vacationer's Guide To Lee Island Coast." Accommodations on the islands usually cost considerably more than those inland. Most importantly for those who bring their own boat, the booklet lists the marinas in the Charlotte Harbor/Pine Island Sound area. There are five marinas on Sanibel and Captiva Islands, 10 on Fort Myers Beach and five in Cape Coral. Pine Island Marina on Pine Island is handy to the sound and the fishing.

Several excellent guides work the area: Kenny Shannon, Venice (813/497-4876), Pete Greenan, Sarasota (813/923-6095), Johnny Walker, Sarasota (813/922-2287), Phil O'Bannon, Fort Myers (813/964-0359), Bill Miller, Charlotte Harbor (813/935-3141), Larry Mendez, Tampa (813/874-3474), Ralph Allen, Punta Gorda (813) 639-0969 and Van Hubbard, Boca Grande (813/697-6944).

10

DIVING THE SHELL COAST

Tim enjoys finding ancient sharks teeth on the Gulf bottom.

Follow the coast road south of St. Petersburg and you'll soon discover Bradenton and then Sarasota, the west coast's version of Palm Beach. The opulent city was started by circus magnate John Ringling, whose fabulous estate is open to the public.

St. Armand's Circle, decorated with statues from Ringling's own collection, is Sarasota's renowned shopping district that attempts to rival Palm Beach's Worth Avenue. Sarasota also boasts particularly good swimming at Lido Beach and Longboat Key.

One of the best kept secrets in all Florida is the tiny village of Boca Grande, situated at the northern point of the perpetually warm and wonderful Shell Coast. Still a winter retreat for millionaires, Boca Grande provides the state's finest tarpon fishing in early spring through July, plus miles of deserted beaches. The old Gasparilla Inn is open only until July, but there are also plenty of rental properties available.

Far better known--and therefore much more crowded--are Sanibel and Captiva Islands, considered two of the best spots in the world for collecting shells. Most of the shells on the beach have been already been picked over, so try looking in shallow water just a few feet out. People bent over while searching for shells are said to be afflicted with a common malady known as the "Sanibel stoop."

The "Ding" Darling National Wildlife Refuge on Sanibel offers a self-drive through hundreds of acres of woodlands; best time to spot wildlife is early or late, not in the heat of the day. Captiva Island, Sanibel's smaller sister isle, has one of the state's most complete resorts, South Seas Plantation, with golf, fishing, scuba diving, sailing school and windsurfing--just about everything you can think of.

When Thomas Edison chose Fort Myers for his winter home, he lamented that one day thousands of people would flock to his uncrowded part of the world. Actually, he is one of the main reasons most tourists visit here, to see for themselves the home and laboratory of America's greatest inventor. The Edison Museum also contains a fine collection of his inventions, everything from light bulbs to phonographs.

Naples boasts more millionaires per capita than any other city in the U.S. Its seven miles of beaches assures visitors of an unspoiled walk along the Gulf. Marco Island, just south of Naples, is the fishing gateway to the Everglades and the best snook fishing grounds in the U.S. To gain a feeling of what life on the fringe of the Everglades was like a century ago, try lunch or dinner at either the 1883 Marco Island Inn or the Marco Lodge (1869), which by Florida standards have been around for quite a long time, indeed.

Going Down, Please

Why all this emphasis on land sites when this is supposed to be a diving chapter? Frankly, hardly anyone visits this region for the main purpose of diving; other places are better.

The offshore bottom has the same characteristic flatness and barrenness of Gulf, and the shallow depths generally require long runs to the diving. Most divers come here for the land sightseeing opportunities. Or they come strictly for the hunting; jewfish seem more prolific here than almost any other part of the state.

Even Southwest Florida, containing some of the state's most bland diving, holds some amazing surprises. Remember, though, the diving season is during spring and summer, when winds are less likely to be a problem.

Perhaps the most intriguing aspect is the chance to find prehistoric shark's teeth belonging to creatures that are a diver's

Bridge pilings anywhere on the Gulf are a good place to search for stone crabs, a great delicacy. But one of the more outstanding sites is the causeway connecting the mainland to the fishing/resort community of Boca Grande.

worst nightmare: monsters from 100 to 150 feet in length, voracious critters capable of literally swallowing a diver whole. Fortunately, these beasts died out millions of years ago, but their fossilized teeth--measuring up to 6 inches--are highly sought prizes. The nice thing about hunting for them, too, is that you don't need a boat. You can simply make a beach dive, a rarity for the Gulf coast.

The best shark teeth finds traditionally have been only 30-40 yards offshore of the Venice Public Beach. This is a flat sandy bottom you need to fan to uncover the prehistoric dentures. For some reason, the best finds are right around the 18-foot level. Visibility at its best is miserable, only 3-4 feet. Don't forget to fly the diver's flag.

Another good shark's teeth hunting area is the Peace River near the small town of Nocatee, over 40 miles west of Sarasota. Best time to search is in winter when the dark water is at its shallowest level and the aggressive gator mating season is over. Using gloves to grub around in the mud bottom, you'll probably find the best hunting in a double bend of the Peace River, 1/4 to 1/2 mile south of the Nocatee Bridge. You should have a boat, even if only a canoe, to hunt here.

● Bradenton Beach also offers a couple of interesting beach dives. The 75-foot Molasses Barge is only a 100 yards out from Trader Jack's Restaurant. It's easy to find: a metal post sticks up from the bow. In calm weather and in only 15-20 feet of water, you'll be surprised at the extent of colorful marine life, particularly sponges. At the intersection of Gulf Drive and 33rd St. is the site known as the Third Pier, the best close-to-shore ledge diving anywhere on the Gulf Coast, only 200 yards out. Depths are only 20-30 feet and best appreciated when the wind is coming from the east, for maximum visibility.

● Moving offshore once again, the Barracuda Hole has more ledges with their typical rocky outcroppings in just 50 feet of water. A popular spot for finding snapper, grouper and amberjack; take a 240-degree heading from the sea buoy at New Pass. At 250-degrees and 11 miles out is the Gully's, another section of ledge from 54-56 feet. Grouper, hogfish, shovelnose lobster and mangrove snappers are typical residents.

● The "Bay Ronto" is a 400-foot German freighter that sank in 1919 in 110 feet of water. The ship is upside down and there are many places to enter the ruptured hull. Large amberjack, jewfish and barracuda live here. This is a challenging dive for the experienced pro. (LORAN: 14140.9/44325.1)

Bridge pilings anywhere on the Gulf are a good place to search for stone crabs, a great delicacy, but one of the more outstanding sites is the causeway connecting the mainland to the fishing/resort community of Boca Grande. The Boca Grande jetties, three rock jetties on the ocean side of the island with 10-12 foot depths, are also a stone crabbers delight.

● Visibility at several of the sites off Fort Myers beach may reach as much as a modest 30 feet. At 197-degrees and 9 miles from the FL G 1 buoy is the misnamed Mud Hole, actually a fresh water spring 40 feet down said to attract large jewfish and sharks. At 240-degrees and 16 miles from the FL G 1 buoy is the rock reef called the "W" in 45-48 feet; another popular spearing ground.

The Naples area, despite all the visitors, sees perhaps the fewest divers of anywhere in the state because of its mediocre visibility and long runs to the limited number of known diving sites.

● The Pinnacles, several steeple-like rock formations that rise 15 feet from the 55-foot bottom, are 22 miles due west of FL G 1 buoy. Another fish attractor is the Mine Sweeper Wreck 200-degrees and 25-miles from the same buoy marker.

The Naples area, despite all the visitors, sees perhaps the fewest divers of anywhere in the state because of its mediocre visibility and long runs to the limited number of known diving sites. The Naples Ledges are 30-40 miles out, consisting of several parallel ridges rising 7-8 feet from the 70-80 foot bottom. Many parts of this are still to be explored. Only 22 miles out is the sunken sinkhole known as The Crater, a 15-foot depression in the bottom that is one of the area's better fish bowls.

● The Black Hole is another sunken sinkhole with a 100-foot wide opening at 65 feet and plunging to 215 feet. The fish life is even better here than at The Crater. (LORAN: 14028.6/43864.2) Four miles north of the Black Hole and testing upside down at 70 feet is the wreck of a 50-foot houseboat. Another good spot for fish watching.

However, to reiterate again, sea conditions make diving Southwest Florida problematical much of the time. Spring and summer are best, but you can almost set your watch by the fierce afternoon summer thunderstorms which typically form inland. Get your diving done early just to be safe.

11

SOUTHWEST PASS AND BEACH TARPON

Larry is among the many anglers who enjoy the seasonal migration of the silver king

In the Lower Gulf Coast area, one fish reigns supreme - the tarpon. While it's not easy to hook a tarpon, much less to land one, the thrill of a strike from the silver king lures many to this area of Florida. From Boca Grande south, the tarpon is King.

Tarpon migrate between fresh and salt water through the passes. In the Boca Grande area, three rivers bring in fresh water. The Myakka River joins the Peace River and flows around the cape. The Caloosahatchee River enters near Sanibel and flows through Pine Island Sound.

Boca Grande is a "stack-up" point for giant concentrations of tarpon. The pass there is deeper and wider than most of the others and the fish will move in and out and run the adjacent beaches. The fishing is best when the tides are strongest and bait movement is greatest, on the full and new moons. In fact, the crabs and shrimp move through the passes all along the lower Gulf coast on those moons.

The clear, deep water in Boca Grande Pass attracts the tarpon during the late spring/early summer spawning season. The tarpon stay in the pass because the extensive forage base is washed to them. When they decide to lay their eggs they go offshore.

Environmental conditions further determine the presence and activity of tarpon in Boca Grande Pass, according to charter boat captain Buster Herzog. When a severe squall packing a lot of lightning comes out of the southeast and hits the pass, most tarpon leave. Charter captains then simply wait for the weather to clear and for the fish to start filtering back into the pass.

Herzog has been guiding for 35 years and has a "tournament-weighed" tarpon of 166 pounds to his credit. His parties have caught and immediately released tarpon that were estimated to be 185 pounds. He knows the tarpon of Southwest Florida.

"When low pressure moves in from the Gulf with a hurricane or tropical storm, the fish move," says Herzog. "The minute the pressure starts dropping, they go to deeper water for safety. If the water is very muddy, such as we have after a southwest wind for several days, they'll turn and leave the pass."

Tarpon don't like the silt in their water from any source. When rainwater flows into the pass from the east, it typically has a lot of tannic acid which affects the fish. The tarpon then usually leave the pass until the water cleans up again. Such a runoff influence might last for a week or two weeks, depending on how much rain fell in the watershed.

Time and Place

The time to chase tarpon in the Boca Grande area is usually between mid April and the end of July for most daylight anglers. The season has started early, though, in the past few years. If the southwest Florida winter is mild, the fish may be in the area in early April. When waters are right then, they are often too hot for the majority of tarpon by the end of June. When the water temperatures reaches 90 degrees, tarpon migrate north toward cooler water. Typically, that occurs in mid to late July.

An ideal water temperature range to find the pass packed with tarpon is 78 to 84 degrees, according to Herzog. An ideal place is the center "boat channel hump" of Boca Grande pass. Tarpon often are wadded up on the hump during a moving tide. When slack tide occurs, they may go elsewhere. Look for them then on the edge, off the beach, at the "V", the southwest ledge, the "hill", or the flats.

The time to chase tarpon in the Boca Grande area is usually between mid April and the end of July.

When fishing the tarpon along the beaches in southwest Florida, a boater has to be very careful when approaching a school of tarpon, according to expert Gulf guide Van Hubbard. If you stop as soon as you see the school of fish, shut off your motor and watch the tarpon to see which way they're going or what they're doing. Then, Hubbard points out that you can intercept them or let them come to you.

97

"You want them to pass around your boat, not just past it," he says. "Then, you want to cast your lure or fly in front of the fish and let the fish move to it. You don't throw into the school of fish; that just scares them. It's not natural for a baitfish to just jump right in the middle of a school of tarpon!"

Beach fishing requires a lot more work and skill than pass fishing. First you have to find the tarpon and get the bait in front of them. After the cast, you have to keep the line tight.

The Backcountry

Some of the fish are migratory and move northward in and out of the creeks and passes with the tides. Guide Phil Chapman fishes for both tarpon and snook in the backcountry area of the upper Ten Thousand Islands south of Marco Island. He concentrates on the creeks, and "sight fishes" for the smaller tarpon. The water visibility in the backcountry where the fish often roll to the surface varies from turbid to clear, to tannic-stained.

Where one rolling fish is spotted, there are usually others, according to Chapman. To connect with one, work the area with streamer flies, plugs or jigs. The fish will often school in or on the edge of the holes, depending on the wind. Look for them in four to 12 feet of water.

The guide prefers to fish light tackle on the outgoing tides in the backcountry, especially if they fall at dawn or dusk. Chapman finds that the small five to 15-pound tarpon love his "Argentina Blond" fly. He ties it on a size 1 hook and uses a 40-pound test tippet.

Larger tarpon can be found on the eight to 14-foot deep flats two miles offshore near White Horse Key or south of Cape Romano. Fish in the normally turbid waters there are not tightly schooled. Plenty of "free-jumpers" denote the presence of tarpon though. Live pinfish or dead mullet work well there.

Luring Attractions

Fly fishing is popular in the lower Gulf Coast area, and an assortment of flies and streamers including locally-produced "Sliders" (weighted flies) work well. MirrOlure plugs and live bait fished on spinning tackle with 12-pound line can also be productive. Vibrating plugs and jigs always take their share of tarpon and snook in the area.

The thrill of a strike from the silver king lures many to Boca Grande.

Most of the professional guides have their clients fish live bait for the tarpon. Due to the high boat traffic, that's the easiest way to fish the pass. Some guides will fish artificial jigs when the boat pressure is not bad. The typical boat pressure in the Boca Grande Pass has influenced the fishing, according to Captain Cappy Joiner.

Fishing squirrel fish for bait used to guarantee a tarpon, but that has changed. Joiner blames it on the boat traffic. During the season, there are as many as 150 boats in Boca Grande Pass, and that's a crowd.

There are so many boats in the pass at times that fishing can be difficult. Some boats new to fishing the pass may cause problems. When you have over 100 boats fishing an area 400 yards by 200 yards, you'd better know how to maneuver your boat and stay out of other fishermen's way. The experienced pass guides are constantly educating newcomers to the pass on the courtesies expected.

"During May and June, there are easily more than 100 boats here 24 hours a day on the weekend," he says. "A falling tide used to be our bread and butter tide, but that too has changed."

Joiner has been a guide at Boca most of his adult life; he was born and raised on Gasparilla Island. He is active in the Boca Grande Fishing Guides Association and pays close attention to the tarpon fishery in the area.

There are fish in the Boca Grande Pass year around, according to Joiner, and as long as the water temperature doesn't get any colder than 65 degrees, the tarpon will stay. That was proven to my wife Lilliam, co-author Tim O'Keefe, and I recently, when we visited the pass one July. The tarpon were still there, past their normal "abandon the pass" time, and our group of eight caught and released 8 tarpon in just three hours. Tim boated three of those fish, weighing up to 65 pounds. If several days of cold temperature occur any time of the year, that will drive the tarpon out of the pass, southward.

Night Opportunities

Tarpon, which feed freely during day light times early in the peak season, resort to more nocturnal activity during the hottest of months. The silver kings are still around off Florida's southern Gulf Coast for those that want to fish for them at night.

Most tarpon stay deep in the passes and feed after dark on small crabs, pinfish, sand perch or large shrimp. Anglers fishing the same on heavy 5/0 hooks rigged to wire leaders take their share. Tarpon guides in the Fort Myers/Boca Grande area drift the passes with heavy line and huge lead sinkers weighing five to eight ounces to keep the bait down in strong tidal currents.

Many visitors prefer to fish later in the evening, from 9 p.m. to midnight to avoid the sun; others know how productive fishing crabs under the moonlight can be. Primarily, the captains fishing the Boca Grande pass area use blue crabs for evening tarpon.

Other nighttime tarpon addicts night-fish from bridges or anchor their boats in the area's shallower rivers and fish cut mullet on the bottom to attract their quarry. With moderate tide movements, their only worry might be the bothersome mosquito and sand gnat populations present in the late summer. Positioning the craft away from the mangrove shores may help keep down the bug bites. (Some good advice: anglers in the back country need to have plenty of insect repellent).

Other Opportunities

● Night trips aboard party boats specializing in snapper fishing out of Fort Myers Beach and Naples are a way to enjoy nocturnal angling experiences. The boats do extremely well on mangrove snapper and yellowtail. The mangroves, ranging from two pounds up to an occasional 10, love to sample live shrimp, sardines or strips of squid.

● Red and black grouper and grunts are numerous about eight miles offshore between Fort Myers Beach and Naples. A sandy bottom with shells and rock ledges in 40 to 60 feet of water attract the fish. Another good spot for grouper, jewfish and cobia is in the same area, just three miles offshore. Called the "Mud Hole," it is a freshwater spring with steep rocky sides in 60 feet of water. It can usually be found from observing its boil of discolored water.

● Bottom fishing for grouper and red and mutton snapper in the summer takes place about 20 miles off Naples in 140 to 180 feet of water. The bottom in the area is sand and shell. Another good spot for red and gag grouper and sea bass is called "245 degrees from Stump Pass." The sandy site has rocks and shell mixed in. In the winter, the bottom fish are caught along the 240 foot contour which is located about 30 miles offshore. "Hambone Ridges" is a good snapper area in 200 feet of water that is defined by a series of ridges on a flat bottom.

● Mangrove snapper are in holes and around the bridges. Trout and snook are in the creeks and canals, and redfish are around the oyster bars and bridges in the spring. Trout and redfish will move onto the grass flats when the waters warm in the summer. Offshore,

101

Spanish and king mackerel are caught in the summer months. In the fall, the two species can be caught in an area called "West of Redfish Pass," which is in 40 feet of water over sand and scattered patches of flat rock.

Boats especially equipped with flood lights for night seatrout angling prowl the lower peninsula's Gulf Coast during August also, and they do well. Bridge and pier fishermen in Southwest Florida also use lanterns and lights to attract baitfish, which in turn bring trout and other fish.

For accommodations, right near the action, contact the Sonesta Sanibel Harbour Resort & Spa, 17260 Harbour Pointe Dr., Fort Myers, FL 33908, or phone (813) 466-4000. Located on the Punta Rasas Peninsula, the 80-acre resort has an old cattle barge sunk at the end of its pier. Snook, redfish, trout and sheepshead are caught right off the pier. Contact the following for guide service: Captain Cappy Joiner, 4634 Arlington Dr., Placida, FL 33946, phone (813) 697-6052; Captain Van Hubbard, P.O. Box 821, Boca Grande, FL 33921, phone (813) 697-6944; Captain Kenny Shannon, 795 Devon Rd., Venice, FL 34293, phone (813) 497-4876. For a booklet on "Tarpon Fishing and Boat Operation at Boca Grande Pass," contact the Boca Grande Fishing Guides Association, P.O. Box 676, Boca Grande, FL 33921.

12

BAYSHORE FLATS AND HIGH FLYERS

Larry can't pass up the action on the flats

World record size tarpon spawn in the spring along the Gulf from Pasco to Citrus Counties. Flats anglers can find the best shallow water action in the crystal-clear waters between Homosassa Bay and Bayport south of Chassahowitzka Bay. For the light tackle angler or fly fisherman, this area offers unsurpassed opportunities to tangle with over-sized silver kings.

Fly rod enthusiasts, in particular, tout the area's quality fishing. They have several good reasons to do so, according to the IGFA record book. Four of the most recent world marks in the fly fishing 16-pound class category were established by Homosassa area tarpon. Most of the 12-pound class fly records set over the past eight years were also taken by anglers converging on the area during the mid to late spring.

The silver giants of record proportions are more abundant in the three to five-foot flats off Homosassa than anywhere else along the Gulf Coast, according to local guide Earl Waters. There are other Florida areas, such as in the Keys, where the numbers of tarpon are greater, but the biggest fish seem to concentrate in the four miles of clear water and white sand bottom between Chassahowitzka Bay and Bayport.

This area is the Fly Fishing Capital of The World. Homosassa attracts most of the world's fly fishing experts, and tarpon guides from all over the state move their operations here from April through mid-June. Many of the state's top tarpon guides move to the best action; they start in Homosassa, and follow the fish as they move southward to the Keys.

It is not uncommon to see schools of a dozen or more of the six-foot long fish moving about the shallows in this area. Tarpon weighing 150 pounds are common and many larger ones have been hooked. All take to the air, and most can leap 6 or 8 feet high. Some of the high jumpers are caught and many escape, but that's the draw for the record chasing anglers. Reports of 200-pound plus silver kings getting off are common each spring.

Fly-tying anglers are frequent visitors to the clear flats north of Tampa. They come to try out their favorite streamers on the powerful hardbodies and, perhaps, to be the first flyfisherman to land a 200-pounder. Winter months are often spent tying a large selection of Deceiver-type and Seducer-type flies onto 1/0 to 3/0 hooks.

The fly experts base their on-the-water selection of flies and fly fishing equipment on the size of tarpon they are likely to encounter. Most opt for No. 8 to No. 10 fly rods and the use of a heavy shock tippet. Tippets testing 100 pounds are well suited for the size of fish normally encountered off Homosassa. The sheer power of most of the 60 to 200 pound armor-plated tarpon would be a challenge on any tackle.

Flats Techniques

The common technique anglers employ around Homosassa is to pole until they locate a school of tarpon. The angler then tries to place a fly or small artificial in front of the fish. Sight fishing demands excellent eyesight and the use of polarized glasses. While the waters are very clear, the depths which vary from three to 8 or 9 feet occasionally make it difficult to see even world-class tarpon.

A slight wind chop lessens the guide's ability to see the fish schools and pods from the poling platform. If the water visibility varies slightly due to rains in the area, the knowledgeable guides will still pick up the fish's gleaming scales and broad tail rolling on the

Calendar - Central Gulf Coast

SPRING	SUMMER	FALL	WINTER
Sailfish	Sailfish	Sailfish	Sailfish
Dolphin	Dolphin	Dolphin	Dolphin
Wahoo	Amberjack	Wahoo	Wahoo
Barracuda	Barracuda	Bluefish	Barracuda
Bluefish	Spanish Mackerel	King Mackerel	Sea Trout
King Mackerel	Sea Trout	Sea Trout	Redfish
Pompano	Whiting	Redfish	Bonito
Spanish Mackerel	Pompano	Snook	
Redfish		Spanish Mackerel	
Snook		Whiting	
Sea Trout			
Grouper			
Snapper			

surface. They realize that while the tarpon won't be as tightly schooled under such conditions, when they see one rolling fish, there are usually others nearby.

Guides also keep their eye out for are the "free-jumpers" that give away the fish's presence. Schools that erupt on the surface as they spook are likewise noted, and a decision is then made to follow or wait a few minutes before poling toward them. Daisy chains, where several fish form a head-to-tail circle, are the ultimate find for the sight fisherman.

Approaching a daisy chain off Homosassa can sometimes be easy. Then again, just as the guide firmly plants his push pole to steady the boat for your cast, the fish will break formation and swim off in the opposite direction of the boat. The silver kings will bolt en masse with the slightest splash-down of a streamer or light plug. At other times, a seemingly-sedentary school may lurk on each side of the boat, calling for a major decision on which way to cast.

Sighting a pod of huge tarpon with easy casting range will get anyone's heart to pumping, so the trick is to sight them and be cool. Slivers of silver plowing dark furrows through the sand seemingly appear and then dissolve before one's eyes. A school being approached sometimes has the uncanny ability to vanish without a trace. More often than not, however, on these flats, scattered pods are noticed during the course of the day.

Tackle and Bait For Trophies

Fly fishermen will then work the schools with streamer flies or a weighted, Florida-produced fly called a "Slider." Many anglers that visit the area, though, are not efficient with the fly fishing gear, so they'll select spinning outfits with 20 pound test line. They toss MirrOlure plugs, vibrating lures and jigs in hopes of a giant hook-up. Red and white, black and silver with blue back are usually productive plug colors, while white and brown bucktail hues are successful enticers.

The Homosassa River dumps thousands of gallons of freshwater into the Gulf each day and such movements over the ragged shellbars near the river's mouth and grassy bottoms nearby enhances foraging activity in the area. Most tarpon in the flats off Homosassa feed on small crabs, pinfish, sand perch or large shrimp, so some anglers opt for such fare.

Live crabs or pinfish fished on 30 to 40-pound test around the boat and river channels are rigged on heavy 5/0 hooks and wire leaders. The live bait is particularly productive in the river itself when a brute wind across the flats forces anglers to try something else for the day.

During the late spring months, it's not uncommon to see several boats in the flats jumping tarpon. They'll have their hands full fighting the fish, and it's up to nearby craft to steer well clear of any involvement. Guides and other locals desire their own little space with no infringements whether they are battling a monster into submission or simply poling after a fast-moving pod.

The flats are sometimes crowded by anglers looking for the giants, but the fishing pressure diminishes in June, and by the end of that month, only a handful of guides and fishermen are there. Tarpon left now may range from 50 to 100 pounds, but fish of such proportions still account for themselves well. When the summer is over, most tarpon have moved back off to deeper waters.

For high-flying action, the time is right. The giant Homosassa silver kings may tear up your prime fly and lure-tossing tackle, but you won't know unless you present them a bait.

Homosassa guide, Earl Waters, pioneered Keys-type fishing for reds from a shallow draft skiff more than a decade ago.

Reds In The Sunset

Redfish feed almost year-round inside the Bay and among the small keys that dot the coastline. Speckled trout show up in the spring and fall and are often taken as an extra bonus, according to Waters.

Lure presentation is critical to attract and to keep from spooking the constantly wary redfish. To be effective, cast the chosen lure about 10 feet beyond the fish, then bring it back in front of its nose.

To provide the best sighting opportunity, Waters approaches each area with the sun behind his client's shoulder. If it clouded up or neared sunset when the sun was too low to offer much illumination, he approaches a likely spot by poling to it from the rear, pushing into the tide since the fish always face into the moving water. Once alongside a mangrove key or limestone ridge, the angler should blind cast across the area, hopefully take a red, then drop back with the tide. That way other fish wouldn't be spooked and there would be the chance to take more from the same location.

"Redfish usually sleep at slack tide, facing into the current, and that's the hardest time to catch them," he explained. "They're most active when the water moves fast, during the last hour of the incoming and outgoing tides. That's when they're holed up behind the shallow limestone ridges, rocks and reeds, waiting to feed on the crabs, crustaceans and baitfish that get caught up in the turbulence. The shallower the water, the faster these baits move, so you can find a lot of reds in only 8-inches of water, just enough to cover their backs."

A two-handed cast achieves greater accuracy. Initially it might feel strange to use two hands--also a surf casting technique--on a light rig, but it is easy to master. The rod is held like a golf club, with the two thumbs pointed in the direction of the cast.

"This method not only provides good projection, you don't have to bring the rod tip farther than the rim of your cap," Waters pointed out. "That's important when two people are fishing next to each other--it prevents you from hooking anyone standing behind."

Lure retrieve is just as simple. The rod tip is pointed toward the water so the spoon doesn't break the surface and scare off a fish. It did take practice to find the proper speed. "A lot of fish will track a spoon but won't strike unless it's the proper speed. Sometimes it helps to slow down and let the fish catch up, then smoke the lure in," Waters suggested. "That's a good way to entice and tease them."

If you want to give it a shot, contact guide Earl Waters at P.O. Box 959, Homosassa, FL 32687; 904/628-0333.

Other Opportunities

Throughout the year, several other species roam the waters from Bradenton to Crystal River. In January, grouper and red snapper can be found in 120 feet of water about 15 miles west of St. Petersburg. Trout are found in the passes and deep-water channels. In Manatee County, sheepshead can be taken around bridge pilings during the winter.

One of the top guides in the Tampa Bay area, Captain James Wood, Sr., put me on my largest Florida snook in the mangrove islands off the Pithlachascotee River at Port Richey. The 33-inch long snook was taken on a 3/8-ounce Cotee Jig and shad tail and put up a classic battle. It swam around the trolling motor a couple of times, tried to bury itself in brush, long strands of grass and clear the water in an attempt to shake the hook.

Tampa Bay area Captain James Wood, Sr., put Larry on his largest Florida snook in the mangrove islands off the Pithlachascotee River at Port Richey.

Wood netted the fish after the tremendous battle; we took a few pictures and released it. For bay and backcountry fishing, contact him at Island "Hop-R" Charter, P.O. Box 224, Terra Ceia, FL 34250 or phone (813) 722-8746.

This entire area has varied fishing in February. You'll usually find trout and redfish in the deep water channels and in rivers and creeks on the west central coast. Black grouper are often taken off Tarpon Springs at a spot in 50 to 70 feet of water. The bottom of sand and shell has rock projections of 12 feet or more. You can find this area 15 miles out in the Gulf. As the water warms, you'll find some trout in the back of Tampa Bay.

In the spring, bottom fishing about 10 west of Clearwater can be productive. A sloping bottom with coral, rock and shell falls off from 80 feet deep. It yields grouper and red snapper. Another hotspot for the species called "245 degrees from Longboat Pass" is in 410 feet of water. Trout and redfish can be found around the Sunshine Skyway Bridge between Palmetto and St. Petersburg.

Good spots for Spanish mackerel in the warmer spring months are the piers. The Big Pier 60 in Clearwater, the Anna Maria City Pier and the pier at Fort DeSoto Park all attract the mackerel. King mackerel can be taken around John's Pass, west of St. Petersburg.

About 20 miles off Bradenton in 90 to 120 feet of water is a sand and shell bottom that has scattered rock and coral which attracts grouper in June. Trout are in the bays and creeks and mangrove snapper are around docks and bridges. July finds numerous grouper actively feeding on the offshore reefs and rock piles near Cedar Key, Crystal River, Homosassa and Bayport. Trout and redfish are usually in the boat channels of Tampa Bay and on the edges of the grass flats and in the passes in August. About 15 miles offshore from Tarpon Springs in 80 feet of water is a good grouper location.

In the early fall, the trout are on the grass flats and the redfish move onto oyster bars. Cobia are found on inshore reefs, around buoys and other structures in the water. Grouper, bluefish and Spanish and king mackerel are offshore. In December, a good grouper spot is about 15 miles offshore between Tarpon Springs and Homosassa. The area of ledges is in 70 feet of water. Mangrove snapper, sheepshead and jack crevalle are in rivers and creeks.

13

PINELLAS FISH & DIVE COAST

Tim explains why both anglers and divers have to frequent the same locations

Gulf Coast anglers and divers face the same difficult situation: the Gulf bottom is mostly a flat, unbroken sandy wasteland lacking the beautiful and prolific reef structures found off the Atlantic coast. It's also shallower; the bottom falls away only 3 feet for every mile. Consequently, fishing and diving trips tend to be fairly long runs, at least a dozen miles or more each way, to find water only 40 feet deep.

Although divers may be completely preservation-minded in other parts of the state, in the Tampa area anglers and divers have identical interests: harvesting gamefish. Both anglers and divers tend to frequent the same sites; only their means of taking fish is different. Gulf coast spearfishermen are considered perhaps the state's finest since hunting is their main underwater activity.

You can even locate lobster here, but more shovelnose and slipper lobsters (sometimes called bastard lobsters) instead of the spiny variety, though they're present, too.

If the Gulf lacks the distinct coral development as the Atlantic (one of the many benefits of the Gulf Stream), it does have a series of unusual bottom formations which do house marine life. One is the series of ledges paralleling the coast which are remnants of Florida's periodic submersions by the sea. These ledges mark the sea level at different periods of history.

111

Dating back thousands of years, these ledges (once shorelines) may rise as little as a foot or as much as 12 feet from the bland, flat bottom. They sometimes extend for miles in a north-south direction. Although they are not considered a true reef system, you will find corals, sponges and similar residents to those of the Atlantic, only not as many or as strikingly prominent.

Generally speaking, the higher and larger the ridge, the better the fish life. Deep pockets that undercut the ledges hold grouper, snook and snapper.

Another interesting bottom formation are the so-called sunken sinkholes, deep depressions in the bottom that are usually tightly packed fish bowls. These depressions may go down hundreds of feet, some of the deepest parts of the Gulf. Divers may get a glimpse of the upper fringes, but it's the line angler who has complete access to the biggest residents of these vertical limestone shafts.

● One of the best known is 32 miles off Tampa, called "Jack's Hole." The 25-foot opening begins at 110 feet but it's anyone's guess how deep the sinkhole goes: its true depth is still unknown. (To locate, take a heading of 225-degrees from John's Pass. Because of the distance, the trip should be undertaken only by boats of 20 feet or more.)

Recognizing that fish inhabit only areas containing some sort of structure, the Gulf has its share of artificial reefs, though they are not nearly as well developed or concentrated as on the Atlantic side. That situation is changing, but it will be quite some time before the Gulf begins to equal the variety found off Miami or the Gold Coast. The artificial reefs consist of sunken ships, concrete culverts, anything likely to attract fish.

● No question about their productivity: the 50-foot deep Pinellas #1 Rube Allyn Artificial Reef yielded the world record cobia of 88 pounds in 1982. (To locate, take a 256-degree heading from entrance marker buoy No. 1 at Clearwater Pass; the artificial reef is 9.8 nautical miles out.)

Gulf Coast Tour

The first area of interest is Cedar Key, a tiny fishing village and artist's colony on the Gulf coast near Chiefland. Deserving of a longer stop is Tarpon Springs, a Greek community just north of

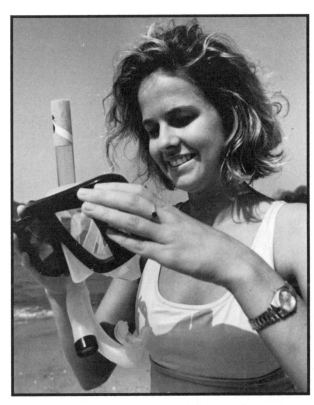

The shallow flats around Tarpon Springs are excellent for snorkelers to harvest one of the sea's great delicacies: scallops.

Tampa that once was the center of Florida's thriving sponge industry. Still quite colorful, Tarpon Springs offers superb Greek cuisine, everything from a leisurely sit-down dining to fast food gyros.

The shallow flats around Tarpon Springs are excellent for snorkelers who have the chance to harvest in summer one of the sea's great delicacies: scallops. You may never have considered a shellfish a migratory species, but scallops do come in from the deep water to the shallower coastal flats, then return as the summer ends. You'll understand how they're able to cover such distance the first time you reach for one and it propels itself away.

Scallopers generally employ an inner tube or raft with nets where they can pile their find but still keep the scallops on ice or in the water. On a successful day, it quickly becomes impossible to

113

snorkel holding a goodie bag of shells. The added weight makes it too easy to get to the bottom, too difficult to get back to the surface.

● Divers have several options, none really overwhelming with one important exception: the wreck of the huge "Meisner Marine Crane," popular with divers from Tarpon Springs to Bayport.

This 250-ton piece of equipment, a Mantiwoc Model 4600 to be precise, was being towed on a barge in December, 1982, from Tampa to the Panhandle. The tug captain in charge of the effort was not deterred by a nasty cold front that whipped the Gulf into 10-12 foot waves. The final result: the crane slipped off the barge and fell in only 49 feet of water. The cab and boom are still totally intact, one of the best fish attractors around. Stone crabs, mangrove snapper, grouper and huge barracuda.

Fishing lines caught on the boom present a potential hazard if you don't carry a knife. Best visibility is in spring, when conditions vary from 30 to 80 feet; a really bad day will only be 15 feet. Currents are sometimes a problem. The wreck is due west of Bayport, 28-30-50N and 83-11-50W.

● Another fish attractor is the Tarpon Springs Artificial Reef 12 miles offshore, ranging from 26-28 feet; a lot of this is concrete culvert. (LORAN: 14259.3/44935.3.

● Pasco County has two artificial reefs 11 and 15 miles west of Gulf Harbor in New Port Richey. Reef PS (LORAN: 14275.4/44997.5) contains four 200-foot barges 11 miles offshore in only 25 feet of water. Lots of excellent spearing for cobia, sheepshead, snapper and flounder. Reef CO (LORAN: 14274.9/45048.6) is 15 miles out in just 30 feet of water. Lots of good marine life, including lobsters.Masthead Ledge rises eight feet from the bottom for 1-1/2 miles, situated 16 miles from bell marker No. 1 in Clearwater Pass; follow a 285-degree reading. Good hiding places for a variety of marine life, and the shelling can be quite good particularly for horse and helmet conch.

● Dunedin Reef is only about 6 miles from Clearwater Pass in 25-30 feet. Buoys pinpoint the northern and southern boundaries. The northern section is near a natural ledge, the southern has a lot of concrete culvert. This is a good game fish attractor. (LORAN: 14247.9/44887.3)

The Ten Fathom Wreck is a 150-foot tramp steamer at 60 feet known for holding some big lobster.

● Clearwater Reef is one of the largest artificial reefs in the area. Marked by four buoys, the depths are only 27-29 feet. Snapper, hogfish and lobster are typical residents. You'll probably see a lot of old tires here: 45,000 of them were dumped here at one time. (LORAN: 14233.3/44851.1)

● The G Marker is a rock ledge only 4-1/2 miles from Clearwater Pass with only 25 foot depths. Yet the marine life can be incredibly good: jewfish, turtles and nurse sharks all have been sighted. Run on a 295-degree heading from bell marker No. 1 in Clearwater Pass.

● The Clearwater Steamer, spilt in half and rising 20 feet from the Gulf bottom, is in 60 feet 23 miles out. (LORAN: 14203.8/44944.9)

● The "Sheridan" in 75 feet of water is a 180-foot tug resting upright; it even still contains its prop. Located 100 yards from the popular "Blackthorn." (LORAN: 14181.9/44941.8)

● The 110-foot Coast Guard cutter "Blackthorn" is one of the Tampa area's most popular wrecks. Not intentionally intended as an artificial reef, it was hit by a freighter in Tampa Bay in 1981, wrecking the hull beyond repair and killing 22 crewmen. It was towed out to Pinellas Artificial Reef No. 2 and sunk. Divers of any ability should be able to enjoy the "Blackthorn." Sitting in 80 feet, it's only 30 foot to the upper deck. The 30-mile run from John's Pass may be a problem for small boaters. (LORAN: 14181.7/44942.6.

● Indian Shores Reef is much closer in, only about 13-1/2 miles from John's Pass. This large artificial reef contains 3 different ships, including vessels of 235 and 240 feet in length, and many pillboxes. (LORAN: 14200.0/44859.7)

● The "Betty Rose" is a 75-foot barge resting upright and intact in 45 feet 10 miles from John's Pass. (LORAN: 14184.3/44769.2)

Treasure Island Reef, in 29-33 feet less than 5 miles from John's Pass, attracts grouper and snapper to its thousand of car and truck tires. Also some fiberglass, pyramid-shaped attractors based on a Japanese design that seems to work quite well; actually, it was the Egyptians who first came up with the idea of pyramid power. (LORAN: 14200.8/44738.7)

● The Ten Fathom Wreck is a 150-foot tramp steamer at 60 feet known for holding lots of hogfish and other edibles. Also some big lobster. Situated 16 miles out from Pass-a-Grille at St. Pete. (LORAN: 14162.3/44755.8)

● The St. Petersburg Beach Reef only 5 miles out in 26-28 feet of water contains sections of the Skyway Bridge, a 200-foot barge and tons of concrete culverts. (LORAN: 14192.9/44694.1)

● Sixteen miles from John's Pass are 3 different sites located not too far apart. The South Jack Wreck contains a large boiler and many scattered pieces over 60 feet (LORAN: 14137.1/44675.0) The South Jack Ledge at 50 feet rises as much as 8 feet high with lots of undercuts known for holding big fish (LORAN; 14163.5/44678.4) The 75-foot long Doc's Barge is split in half but otherwise pretty much intact on a 225-degree heading from John's Pass.

● The 65-foot shrimper "Gunsmoke" is one of the areas best dives, listing starboard in only 80 feet. A drug runner carrying bales of pot, she was scuttled while being chased by the Coast Guard. Be mindful of the shrimp nets on the rigging. (LORAN: 14143.6/44762.4)

14

SPACE COAST
ANGLING VARIETY

Larry frequently explores the coast from Melbourne to Titusville

The plastic worm touched down softly ahead of the school, and guide Shawn Foster started to twitch the fare back over the grass-spotted sand. A big redfish met the morsel and boiled on the hook set. It took off across the shallow flats toward the Eau Gallie causeway against Shawn's screaming drag.

"That's a double" he shouted, as I also started my battle with a twin of Shawn's 15 pounder. "Cast to the far edge of that nervous water, Dave," shouted Shawn to my fishing buddy. " The school's moving that way."

The guide tried to head off the school and get Dave into a share of the action. That, however, was at my expense. My redfish was towing out drag in a westerly direction while the school he was trying to stay with was heading east.

"Running low on line," I yelled to our captain whose foot was firmly planted on the trolling motor "on" button.

"You two just work on your double," Dave offered. "I'll have my chance again shortly."

Five minutes later, Shawn's hook pulled free, and about five minutes after that, I landed mine. We quickly posed for a few photos and watched the red gently swim off. Shawn nosed his bass boat back around toward the shallower reaches of the Banana River flat.

117

It wasn't long before Dave caught a nice trout from the grass stretch in three feet of water. Shawn again hooked a red near the point of some mangrove-type trees, but this fish was much larger than our initial two strikers. While he tried to control the boat so that Dave and I had an additional opportunity casting at the school of reds, Shawn's fish had other ideas. His battle continued as the big red moved toward deeper water and pulled us behind.

Dave and I continued to cast the deeper portions of the flats as Shawn's attention was now fully on his adversary. Some 15 minutes later, the 25 pound red was guided into Dave's waiting net. I took a few photos and that fish glided off sans the plastic worm and hook.

Our action that morning on new plastic baits, called Jerk Worms, continued as we boated another three reds between 8 and 25 pounds. One of the highlights was watching a huge school of about 100 redfish between 10 and 15 pounds move right under and around our boat. We had a double on during that pass, and I lost mine at the boat after about 15 minutes of great battling fun.

The air temperature was about 85 degrees that day and the water temperature was 80, just right for some big fish battles. Spicing up the redfish action were eight trout ranging up to about two pounds, an errant lady fish and a couple of catfish. All were caught on the six-inch plastic bait off the extensive flats areas between the Eau Gallie Causeway and the Highway 520 Causeway at Cocoa.

The guide had found the waters about 2 1/2 to 3 feet deep to offer abundant redfish and trout. Shawn has taken several redfish over 40 pounds on spoons and soft plastic worms. His largest, a 50-pounder, was 28 inches in girth and 56 inches in length, taken on an ultralight, medium-action bass rod, 10 pound test line and 15 pound leader. The fish gave him the battle of his life and took over five hours to land.

"The fish hit the bait in just over a foot of water and went right by the boat," he relates. "I had caught a 40-pounder on a fly rod the year before so I knew I was in for a battle. This 50-pounder went six miles from one end of the river all the way across and then back again. After 1 1/2 hours on high speed, the trolling motor batteries were used up. The fish was still taking off more line, so I went to the big motor and just chased after it."

The flats today are a natural feeding ground for redfish, and because there is no longer netting for redfish, the fishery has been restored.

Shawn used up 3/4 of a tank of gas in the following 3 1/2 hours before landing the 50 pound red. That fish was taken in September, just as the weather was starting to change. The week before, Shawn had seen lots of large reds pushing water around the Satellite Beach area, so he was not surprised at its size. Later, in February, he and a client caught one red estimated at about 35 pounds and four others which each weighed 27 or 28 pounds.

119

Color Me Green

We were using three different bait colors to catch our fish. "Arkansas Shiner," a dark green with a silver metallic belly, the "Green Wienee," which is bright green with orange flecks in it, and a black back with silver pearl belly color.

The worms are effective because they resemble one of the primary baitfish, a needlefish. The coloration of our baits and their shape were similar to the natural forage. When twitched across the newly emergent grass patches on the sandy flats, the bait's movement also resembles that of the needlefish.

The greenish colors also mimicked the hues of other baitfish that share the grass flats in the intracoastal waterway such as shiners, greenies and even finger mullet. When we experimented with some of Dave's more flashy colors that day, such as Blue Smoke or Chocolate Mint, we didn't find them to be as effective as those colored green. Numerous schools of mullet typically roam the flats, so Shawn doesn't change colors often.

That day, we also saw plenty of sting rays on the flats, the ever-present pelicans and the tell-tale sign of reds, the porpoise. In fact, Shawn specifically looks over the flats for schools of porpoises because redfish tend to follow the mammals as they move through a shallow area, stirring it up.

Sign of the Intracoastal Flats

"The signs I look for are bait skipping and the presence of porpoise feeding," he explained. "These big reds tend to follow the porpoise and pick up on their scraps. Because the reds are so large, the porpoise leave them alone. Probably about 30 percent of the time, redfish will be a couple of hundred yards behind the porpoises."

"If the water is calm, I'll look for big wakes," the captain continued. "When I'm using the trolling motor or large outboard and all of a sudden the water wells up, that means there are fish there."

If the redfish have been pressured by several boats working the flats, Shawn finds them to be spooky. Even then, he is often able to get behind the school, put his trolling motor on high speed and generally get within casting range when the fish begin to slow down. The Cocoa Beach captain uses his trolling motor about 90 percent

Calendar - Central Atlantic Coast			
Spring	Summer	Fall	Winter
Amberjack	Amberjack	Sailfish	Sailfish
Dolphin	Dolphin	Dolphin	Dolphin
Sailfish	Sailfish	Wahoo	Wahoo
Wahoo	Sea Trout	Marlin	Marlin
Cobia	Tarpon	Redfish	Barracuda
Flounder	Spanish Mackerel	Tarpon	Redfish
Sea Trout	Flounder	Snook	Cobia
Redfish	Redfish	Amberjack	Sea Trout
Snook (3 only)	Grouper	Sea Trout	Tarpon
Tarpon	Snapper	King Mackerel	Grouper
Pompano	Cobia	Grouper	Snapper
King Mackerel	Wahoo	Cobia	Blackfin Tuna
Bluefish	Bluefish	Flounder	Spanish Mackerel

of the time when working the flats. His outboard is used only when the distance between areas or points is far.

At certain times of the year, he may do considerably more searching than finding. In the cool winter months, fish on the flats are generally spooky and on the move, according to Shawn. He's not exactly sure why, but believes it may be because they're searching for baitfish, and there is just not much forage available in the flats.

Shawn has caught big redfish from several areas in the Banana and Indian Rivers. Some of his favorite spots are the Satellite Beach flats, either the east or west bank of the Pineda flats (near the Pineda Causeway), the east bank flats between Patrick Air Force Base and the Highway 520 Causeway. Another good area for catching reds is the Titusville flats near the Nassau Causeway. In fact, most of the grassy flats between Titusville and Melbourne are subject to schools of redfish taking up temporary residence, according to the guide.

Fishery Discovery
It was just a few years ago when Shawn first discovered the redfish fishery in those flats. He was fishing for trout and noticed some porpoise feeding. Behind the big mammals were some smaller fins that weren't baby porpoises. They were giant reds, and that first school had probably 400 fish in it with none under 25 pounds.

121

"That was in September of 1989 and those fish stayed for a couple of months and left during the cold months," says Shawn. "When we have cold, windy weather and the water temperatures are below 62 degrees, the reds move off to deeper water. After a few days of warming weather, the fish will move onto the flats to warm themselves up."

"They seem to be showing up earlier every year; it's getting to be like they once were many years ago before netting pressure became too great. Because of the netting pressure then, they never managed to make it to these areas."

Shawn believes that the flats today, as they once were, are a natural feeding ground for redfish, and because there is no longer netting for redfish, the fishery has been restored. His best day on redfish caught and released has been eight of the giants which ranged from about 22 pounds up to one estimated at 46. On the flats, the big reds tend to school by size. The 40-pounders will be with 40-pounders.

Schooler Activity

There are probably three sizes of schools of redfish using the flats between Titusville and Melbourne, according to the captain who guides redfish anglers about half of his 150 days on the water annually. Some are the mammoth size between 35 and 50 pounds, others are in the 8 to 10 pound class and still others are between 12 to 20 pounds. Number-wise, the schools will vary from about 10 fish up to ones comprised of 400 or 500 fish.

The reds can often be found around points and creek channel mouths, at the opening of small bays and over shallow grass bed areas. The points are usually better early in the morning and again later in the afternoon. Grass beds with numerous patches of sand that are close to water about a foot deeper than the surrounding flats is ideal.

"You will do well if you can find them laying down, which is the term we use for a fairly stationary school," Shawn advises. "Then when you run into them, they generally won't spook much. They'll just swim off slowly, and that's the chance for everyone to hook up."

"In summer, the reds here are easier to approach because as the water temperature warms up, they save their energy and tend to feed at night more," he says. "When you locate them early in the morning, you'll tend to find them finning. They will be relatively still and their fins and tails will be very easy to find because they're so big."

Once you find a school of reds on the flats, if you don't get any radical weather changes for a few days, you have a better than 50/50 chance of finding them for several days, according to Shawn. As spring rolls into summer, the numbers of fish probably quadruple. Several schools will join up and then separate on the flats. Shawn once located three separate schools on the flats that, if they would've gotten together, would have totaled over 1,000 fish.

To hook up with some reds, contact Shawn Foster at 105 LaRiviere Road, Cocoa Beach, FL 32931; phone 407/784-2610.

Mosquito Lagoon

Mosquito Lagoon's flats are several miles wide by 20 miles long. Surrounded by the thick mangroves of Merritt Island National Wildlife Refuge and the Canaveral National Seashore, its name is an apt one. Except in the roughest weather, the water is quite clear thanks to the filtering action of the immense grass beds.

But it takes the right kind of fishing craft to work this area. Sightfishing for reds is best in water that's three feet or less. Redfish are present year-round, but the season really begins in late March or April when the shallow flats start to warm up. Fishing tends to slow in the overheated months of July, August and early September, when the shallow water temperatures can reach a daytime average of 90 degrees.

Fishing picks up again from mid-September until the first hard cold snap, which usually comes in November when the fish disperse to deep holes in the lagoon. If you can locate those holes, you may find whoppers of 35 and 40 pounds. In spring and gall, speckled trout are sometimes taken as a bonus while redfishing, though trout generally prefer silver spoons over gold.

Although tidal flow is an important consideration for catching reds in many regions, it's a negligible factor in Mosquito Lagoon where there is virtually no tidal movement. (The water does fluctuate but mostly due to runoff from heavy sustained rains.) Without having to contend with a tide schedule, you can fish according to your designs, not nature's. So angling is effective any time of day.

Despite the superb redfish, Jon Cave is one of the few guides who fishes Mosquito Lagoon regularly. For more information or to book a trip, contact him at, 1623 Hastings Court, Casselberry, FL 32707; toll free 800/932-REEL or 407/696-6119.

Other Opportunities

Trout are on the grass flats of the Mosquito Lagoon and in the Indian and Banana Rivers (Intracoastal Waterway) in spring and summer. The really big trout are often taken in the fall from the same areas. When cold weather hits, they pile into the deep canals and channels. Sheepshead and drum are usually caught around the bridge pilings of the causeways as well.

Not all of the action between Sebastian Inlet, south of Melbourne and Titusville is inshore. Sebastian, in fact, is one of the best inlets for big snook and a variety of other species. The surf and inlets in this region offer excellent fishing for bluefish, whiting, croaker, pompano and jack crevalle. These fish are also caught from the piers along the coast.

Anglers from Melbourne and Vero Beach take Highway A1A to the inlets for some fishing that is typically "flat." The inlet yields some monster "door mats" which weigh up to 14 pounds. Flounder angling doesn't get any better that. Large tarpon can be found in the cooler months along some beaches and in some inlets where large mullet schools are running.

Out in the Atlantic at the Gulf Stream, the offshore sailfish action runs hot and cold. A dozen sails caught and released out of the inlet on one weekend is not an unusual occurrence for mid-August. King mackerel and bonito add to the normal summer and fall action found here. Dolphin hang tight to the weedlines, and can provide some exciting action also.

In the past few years, wahoo have also been active in the same areas, in 360 feet of water. They should put in an appearance off Port Canaveral and Vero Beach in the summer. Wahoo from 50 to 90 pounds have been taken off Central Florida's east coast. Cobia and tuna join the wahoo to provide some excitement to those that work the offshore blue waters some 12 to 15 miles out.

Out in the Atlantic at the Gulf Stream, the offshore sailfish action runs hot and cold.

Bottom fishing can be good during the summer months. One of the top spots for red and vermilion snapper, red grouper and trigger fish is called "73-Foot Ridge." It is a coral reef located about 15 miles east of the Melbourne coastline. Depths here run from 73 to 84 feet. Another popular bottom fishing spot is located about 10 miles off Cape Canaveral and is called "Party Grounds." The bottom attraction is a six-foot cliff that runs for about one-half mile. Yet another hot spot for snapper and grouper is found about 10 miles southeast of Port Canaveral in 210 to 300 feet. The ridge of irregular rock lies parallel to the 100-fathom curve.

15

ATLANTIC COAST DIVING

Tim reveals where to view exciting marine life.

Once again, this is an extensive area for diving that receives little publicity or acclaim compared to its land counterparts. For diving purposes, the Central Florida region starts at Jupiter bordering the northernmost border of South Florida, and continues to Daytona Beach. That's not only a lot of square miles, it's an abundance of good diving that usually only the locals know about.

Jupiter, Vero Beach, Stuart and Fort Pierce are particularly noted for their excellent deep sea fishing. The entire Indian River region is noted for its oranges and grapefruit which are shipped worldwide. Cocoa Beach has long been the gateway to the Kennedy Space Center and Cape Canaveral, yet it rarely receives large crowds except at launch time. Spaceport USA at the Kennedy Space Center may be Florida's best tour bargain. Except for the big-screen IMAX movie and the guided bus ride out to the gantries, all the exhibits--including the chance to view a piece of moon rock--are free.

Two of Florida's best--and least known--natural attractions are at Titusville, just north of the Spaceport. The Canaveral National Seashore is a 20-mile stretch of pristine Atlantic beach, the longest natural beach remaining on the state's east coast. It's popular for hiking, fishing, surfing and just plain sunning. The Merritt Island National Wildlife Refuge offers a self-guided drive-through of thousands of acres of marshlands that are home to alligators, scores of bird species and many endangered animals.

Known as "The World's Most Famous Beach," Daytona in spring is a key migration center for college students from the country over. The rest of the year, Daytona belongs more to families and locals, so don't be put off by Easter-time photos of frenzied teenagers.

Daytona Beach is 23 miles long and, at low tide, is 500 feet wide. Inland, the Daytona International Speedway is one of the hottest tracks in the country in late June and early July with the Paul Revere 250 and the nationally famous Firecracker 400 Ponce Inlet, just south of Daytona, is headquarters for several party boats that fish the offshore reefs. The seafood restaurants at the Inlet are excellent.

Wet Dreams

Since Florida's true reef system ends in the Broward County area, East Central Florida diving consists mostly of ledges, ship wrecks and artificial reefs. That's very similar to what is off the Central Gulf Coast, but the Central Atlantic tends to be a lot richer in marine life, particularly spiny lobster.

● The 459-foot amphibious assault ship "USS Rankin" is one of the east coast's largest artificial reefs. Sunk in 1988, the main deck is only 80 feet deep. Located 6 miles southeast of the St. Lucie Inlet. (LORAN: 14373.1/61986.7)

● Looking for another wreck close in? The 147-foot tanker "Esso Bonaire III" is at 90 feet only 4 miles from the Jupiter Inlet. (LORAN: 14351.3/62006.5)

● South of Jupiter inlet and beginning just a half mile offshore are a series of ledges known for holding lobster, grouper and tropicals. If you're lucky, you may even see a ray. Because of current, these sites--The Ranch, Barrow Reef, Reformation Reef, Jupiter High Ledge, Rio Jobe Reef and Juno Ball Ledge--are best regarded as drift diving locations. East 1-1/2 miles of Jupiter Inlet is the Grouper Hole, a ledge paralleling the shoreline at 70-80 feet. The name Grouper Hole comes from the many grouper that may take refuge here during the winter migration.

● The tanker "Gulf Pride" is only a mile from the Jupiter Inlet in 40 feet. Split in two and on the bottom since WWII, visibility can be poor when the winds are up; wait for calm. Good fish and marine life. (LORAN: 14351.9/62026.2)

● Six Mile Reef, which happens to be 6 miles from the St. Lucie Inlet at an 80-degree heading, is a ledge at 75-80 feet where you'll often encounter a current flowing north. Snapper and grouper don't seem to mind it.

● Beach diving is possible at several spots around Jupiter and Vero. Blowing Rocks, 2 miles north of the Jupiter Inlet on A1A, gets its name from all the wave activity in high winds; an easy dive when calm, the ledges hold a good amount of fish life, including snook. The North Jetty Reef at the St. Lucie Inlet offers a drift dive over shallow ledges from 4 to 20 feet. Snook and lobster are often present.

● At the south end of Hutchinson Island is the old House of Refuge, a museum that was once an active station to aid seamen whose craft went down off area shores. A 100-yard swim from the south end of the concrete wall in front of the museum will put you on the ribs of an old schooner. Keep an eye out for sand dollars on the swim out. The public beach at the south end of MacArthur Rd. on Hutchinson Island offers a popular snorkeling site known as Bathtub Reef.

● Toilet Bowl Reef, 3-1/2 miles from the St. Lucie Inlet, is so appropriately named: it consists of old toilets dumped to form an artificial reef. You may never have wondered before about the fate of old toilets, but now you know. Sunken barges are also at the site. (LORAN: 43107.3/62013.1)

● The Fort Pierce region also contains some good beach and wreck dives in addition to some excellent hunting for big lobster. One of Florida's finest WWII shipwrecks is 13 miles from the Ft. Pierce Inlet: the freighter "Halsey" torpedoed by a German U-boat is broken into 3 sections, but the bow and stern section still sit upright. (LORAN: 43175.7/61987.0)

● Another WWII war victim is the freighter "Amazon," also known as the 12A Wreck. The ship, scattered over the 100-foot bottom, has long been an excellent fish attractor. (LORAN: 43206.1/61975.3)

● The Fingers is probably the area's best reef dive, a series of ledges extending for 10 miles known for such healthy marine life it's sometimes referred to as a Keys-like experience. Look for snapper, grouper and excellent photo conditions; 12 miles off the Ft. Pierce Inlet at a 60-degree heading. A mile north of the inlet is a good fish watching station, the Old South Bridge in 30-40 feet of water. Lots of fish but few lobster.

● Beach diving at Ft. Pierce is also uncommonly good. Jaycee Park, 1-1/2 miles south of the inlet on A1A, contains a set of three shallow ledges between 100-300 yards of shore. The depth varies considerably from the inner to the outer rock strip. You'll encounter the first ledge at 15-20 feet, the second at 25-30 and the final ledge from 55-60 feet. Good for shelling and lobstering.

● Inlet Park at the southern end of the Ft. Pierce Inlet is another good shore dive but watch for boat traffic on weekends. Ledges as shallow as 15-30 feet parallel the shore only 75 yards out. Another favorite lobstering and fish watching spot. Two miles north of the inlet on A1A is another public park, Pepper Park, with ledges forming only 100 yards from the beach. Depths range from 15-30 feet. Lobstering is allowed but spearing is prohibited. Finally, the wreck of a Civil War paddle wheeler rests on the sand bottom just 100 yards from the beach. Its ribs and boiler still prominent, this is a popular hangout for tropicals. Located .9 mile south of the Bryn Mawr Campground on A1A. You can spot the ship from shore on a calm day.

Beach Diving Capital

So, you're an independent diver who likes to be away from the crowds but don't own a boat. Vero Beach is tailor-made for you. Four reef lines run parallel to shore; the two in closest are the least interesting because of their low profile and partial coating of sand. The deeper ledges are higher profile still within 200 to 400 feet of the beach with depths amazingly shallow, from 10-30 feet. This is the closest beach diving to Orlando and Disney World.

Visibility attains 25 feet of calm days; high winds make this a potentially dangerous place to dive. It was here that the 1715 Spanish Silver Plate Fleet broke up on the reefs, scattering silver and gold, cannon and ballast stone all over the bottom which were

Pelican Flats is a massive region of limestone ridges at about 80 feet, 22 miles out. This is also a popular spot because of the many snapper and shark.

not discovered until the 1950s. Coins are still found on the beaches by those with metal detectors, and you may even spot some ballast rock. It is illegal to use a metal detector inside the park boundaries.

While looking for treasure, keep an eye out for the valuable spiny lobster which grow to quite large size in this area. Incidentally, most locals don't try and swim out to these sites but use inflatable boats. Swimming is quite feasible at many spots.

● For instance, Round Island's reef is only 150 feet out in 15 feet of water. This public beach is located 5 miles south of the 17th St. Bridge on A1A. Situated off 17th Street is the high profile Cove Reef (ledges 15-20 feet high) about 400 yards from shore, which is a bit of a swim. An inflatable would be better.

● At the end of Riomar Drive near the Riomar Beach Club is, amazingly enough, Riomar Reef. Several cannon from the 1715 fleet should still be here. The reef varies from 10 to 500 feet from the shore with depths of 3-20 feet.

● Humiston Beach is a sizable public beach with lifeguards and the other trappings of a highly-visited location. Located off Ocean Drive, all four ledges are swimmable here, from 100 to 400 feet out.

● The pretzel remains of the 200-foot steel ship "Breconshire" which went down in 1894 are covered with marine growth at 15-20 feet. She's located at the east end of SR-60; her boiler breaking the surface makes an easy landmark.

● A mile north from SR-60 on Ocean Drive are the mile-long Jaycee and Conn Way Beaches. The ledges, up to 8-10 feet high, begin just 200 feet out; depths usually max out at around 20 feet. The Tracking Station is another public beach with reeflines also starting about 200 feet offshore. The bottom here is very rocky. Located on A1A 2-1/2 miles north of the A1A/SR-60 intersection.

● Heading into Indian Shores on A1A is a public beach with access roads at both the southern and northern ends. Diving begins on the ledges just 150 feet out with a second reefline starting at 100 yards offshore. Good for lobster and other marine life. Another good spot is at the town of Wabasso. Its beach provides boardwalk access and the numerous ledges begin just 75 feet from shore; depths vary from 6-15 feet.

● Sebastian Inlet State Recreation Area, one of Florida's most-visited parks, offers the chance to learn about the 1715 treasure fleet at its McLarty Museum. One mile south of the bridge is the opportunity to see the remains one of the ships, the "El Capitan." The shallow depths, only 2-20 feet, should be avoided during active seas. The reef containing several of the ship's cannon and scores of ballast stones begins just 20 feet offshore, an incredible opportunity. Visibility won't be outstanding, but it's not as far as the Keys, either.

● Port Canaveral is the deepwater entry to the Atlantic for the communities of Titusville and Merritt Island, typically referred to as the Space Coast. In contrast to the above listings, all the diving is far offshore; lobstering and hunting are the main activities. Sometimes the competition with line anglers can be intense. This is not a heavily dived region.

● Pelican Flats (LORAN: 43780.7/61930.4) is a massive region of limestone ridges at about 80 feet, 22 miles out. This is also a popular spot for the fishing party boats because of the many varieties available, including snapper and shark. The 148-foot freighter

"Damocles" (LORAN: 43866.0/61920.0) sits upright in 85 feet of water 10 miles offshore. Part of an artificial reef project sunk in 1985, you'll also find lots of concrete culverts scattered nearby.

● Three ships torpedoed by German submarines in 1942 give testimony of the free hand the U-boats had during the early days of WWII at sinking ships whenever and wherever they liked off the Florida coast. The freighter "Ocean Venus," better known as the "Lead Wreck," is 17 miles offshore at 70 feet and a profile of 36 feet. (LORAN: 43859.0/61926.3)

● The 400-foot "Laertes" is a broken heap 11 miles out, resting at 72 feet with a profile of 28 feet. (LORAN: 43931.9/61940.7) And the 200-foot freighter "Leslie" 21 miles out rests at 80 feet. (LORAN: 43972.1/60884.5) A wreck of much older vintage is the wooden steamship "City of Vera Cruz" caught in a fierce storm in 1880; 68 crewmen died. The broken remains extend a hundred yards at 80 feet and still yield interesting artifacts. (LORAN: 44067.6/61910.2)

Greater Daytona

This may claim to be the world's 'most famous beach, but there isn't any beach diving. Like Port Canaveral, the boats going out of the Ponce DeLeon Inlet must travel up to 20 miles offshore. Hunting and lobstering are the main activities, which the weather typically limits to the calmer summer periods. Visibility ranges from 25-75 feet. Diving often Daytona is often referred to as "adventure diving" because of the challenging conditions much of the year. All distances provided refer to the run to the dive site from the marker at the mouth of Ponce Inlet.

● Daytona's best easy dive is the 446-foot long "Mindanao," a Liberty ship sunk in 1980 by the Halifax Sport Fishing Club. Resting in only 80 feet, this 3-decked craft rises to within 50 feet of the surface. Large holes cut in the sides allow access for divers and fish life to the crew's quarters and engine room. The huge ship is intact except for the rupture across its hull from colliding with the bottom. The bow points north. (LORAN: 44453.8/61982.3)

● Rainbow Reef is the lyrical name for a bunch of concrete culverts placed over a 2500-square foot area in 1987. And old houseboat also rests here in the 73-78 foot depths almost 17 miles offshore. (LORAN: 44519.4/61959.1)

133

● If conditions make the boat ride endurable, 50 miles offshore is the "Freighter Wreck," a Liberty ship torpedoed during WWII. It still carries its full cargo of Jeeps and other war materials. Diving here is hampered by the strong currents which make artifact collecting and hunting sometimes impossible. (LORAN: 44149.0/61795.8)

● Turtle Mound is an unmarked reef at 60-70 feet with ledges rising as much as 10-12 feet, located 23 miles out. (LORAN: 44257.4/61917.2) Another large reef area with slightly smaller ledges is East Eleven, known for its shell collecting and big schools of fish; another long run, almost 20 miles out. (LORAN: 44327.2/61927.3) Man-made Culvert Reef consisting of tons of culvert pipe at 80 feet is 12 miles out. (LORAN: 44396.3/61972.8)

● Big fish such as cobia, grouper and snapper are the order of the day at the Party Grounds, 18 miles off the coast. Easily identified at its southern and northern edges with markers that say "PG," this is a popular spot for party boats. (LORAN: 44390.2/61925.8) So are the North East Grounds 13 miles offshore with depths of 80-85 feet. (LORAN: 44432.8/61932.0) "Cracker Ridge," composed of dumpsters, a barge and car transport trailers are at 80 feet about 13 miles out. (LORAN: 44409.1/61959.0)

● Stephen Crane, author of the "Red Badge of Courage," is believed to have been a passenger aboard the small ship known as the "12 Mile Wreck." The ship, because of all the scattered ammunition for Gatling guns, is said to have been a gunrunner during the Spanish-American War. Conditions can be beautiful here during summer: good visibility and spadefish, jewfish and amberjack. (LORAN: 44281.2/61736.6)

● Two more artificial reefs of note: Nine Mile Hill made up of old cars, tires and concrete pilings (LORAN: 44473.4/62035.3) and the Port Orange Bridge Rubble scattered in 75 feet of water in 1989 (LORAN: 44437.8/62020.0) Although in quite different directions, both reefs are approximately. 7 miles from Ponce DeLeon Inlet.

Although water temperatures certainly warm up considerably in summer, a light wet suit in summer is not a bad idea for diving the Daytona region.

16

FISHING THE
SPEEDWAY COAST

Larry waits for summer to fish off Daytona. Bottom fish, billfish, wahoo and other sportfish all move shallower and become more active in the warmer months off the Daytona coast. As the summer progresses, kings and other offshore fish move in, giving area anglers a broad choice. The extremely close-in bottom fishing off Daytona Beach may slow down a little on the shallow reefs during the hottest times. Wise anglers then will just anchor up and travel a few extra miles to deeper water.

Most of the year, bottom fishing off Daytona Beach is a near-shore opportunity that many can't resist. When warm weather arrives, grouper, snapper and other bottom fish are a little closer to the beach. Add to that the potential of a bruising king-size jack crevalle or amberjack and you have the makings for some excitement.

Sport fishermen usually have to run 20 or 30 miles each way for action, and so do bottom fishermen during the colder months. In summer, though, if there's a small rock around, it will attract schools of red snapper, and they'll hit a variety of baits. In the winter, few anglers fish the close-in areas for snapper because they just won't bite, according to local party boat captains.

Fortunately, finding the better bottom fishing areas is not too difficult. The Daytona Beach Halifax Sport Fishing Club has produced a chart for the area that has a listing of all the wrecks and

135

reefs, and the compass headings to get there. Due to local interest in helping anglers catch fish around Daytona, there aren't many secret spots or fishing methods.

Plenty of forage exists on and around the reefs, and that keeps the angler's quarry abundant. Lobsters are favorite fare of the large bottom fish, while small dolphin are the normal delicacy for large sport fish. The shallowest reefs around the Daytona Beach area are in 60 feet of water, but the majority of the better ones lie in at least 90 feet of water or deeper.

The 11-fathom reef about 20 miles offshore is where most of the bottom fishing takes place. The reefs stretch down to Cape Canaveral and up to St. Augustine. A fleet of 20 to 30 offshore craft, both private charter and party boats, frequently leave their berths in the Ponce de Leon Inlet area and head for the area to bottom fish.

One area along that reef line, called "Red Snapper Sink," is reportedly a fresh water spring. According to one local captain, Germans submarines came there during World War II to refill their fresh water tanks. It lies in about 90 feet of water off Flagler Beach and offers numerous grouper and snapper. An occasional billfish may also be found cruising the waters nearby.

The hot months are the time to chase any species of bottom dweller off Daytona. In the winter, the better fishing is some 70 miles northeast at the St. Augustine Inlet.

Reef Runners

● Summer bottom fishing includes areas like Pocket Reef which consists of piles of cement culverts. Local officials started dropping the cement there a few years ago, and they're still adding to it. The reef, located about 15 miles out, holds amberjacks and smaller bottom fish in water 70 feet deep.

● The Northeast Grounds is a popular grouper spot about 15 miles offshore. Another good amberjack area are the WW II airplanes sunk approximately 28 miles northeast of Ponce Inlet in about 70 feet if water. That's a particularly good area for bottom fishing, where you'll also find king mackerel. Electric reels are seldom used on Ponce Inlet charters, so the cranking can be tough.

● The locally-famous "Party Grounds" consist of two dozen or so reefs all within the cruising range of a 20-foot boat. The excellent

Some of the most popular offshore fishing spots are located between 12 to 15 miles out from Inlet Harbor.

fishing reefs are located 17 miles offshore and extend for almost 25 miles. The Party Grounds probably produce more bottom fish than any of the other reefs around the area. Schools of king mackerel are abundant in those waters, as are grouper and red snapper around the natural reef in 90 feet of water.

The kings are found in 90 to 100 feet of water on out to the edge of the stream. Ballyhoo, trolled behind a feather, produce kings in the colder months. Farther out, it's usually rough-water fishing in the winter, and that favors larger boats.

● Other productive bottom fishing areas for red and black grouper, snapper, sea bass, and redeye are the Half North reef, which lies 22 miles offshore, the 80-foot deep "East Ridge" rock reef located about 22 miles out, and Coral Mound. One popular red snapper and grouper spot is located 25 miles off New Smyrna Beach in 140 to 200 feet of water. The rocky reef has a number of holes in it. One just 15 miles off New Smyrna Beach is a two-mile long coral ridge in 70 to 80 feet of water called "East 11 Grounds."

The wrecks in the area also offer good fishing, but are sometimes fished out. Some of the more popular were purposely sunk for

137

fishing and are located between 12 to 15 miles out. There are others farther offshore. The 28-fathom wreck is composed entirely of dilapidated Army jeeps and trucks. Bottom fishermen can catch grouper, jewfish, amberjack, dolphin and wahoo on the wreck, and the trolling anglers may also catch billfish around it.

● "The 28-fathom wreck is one of the best all around fishing areas off Daytona," a local captain told me. "The wreck hasn't yielded any significant records, just good all around fishing."

Spanish mackerel can be found just one or two miles offshore from the Daytona beachfront all summer long. In late June and early July, local anglers and charter boats catch a lot of smoker kings 20 pounds or bigger with live baits. The best area may be right around the bell buoy near the beach. Productive anglers drift live pinfish on a wire leader for best results.

Offshore Big Game Fish Options

The Daytona Beach area offers excellent, and often overlooked, billfishing waters. It can be a hot area for catching billfish, if you don't mind running a ways for them. Most often the sailfish and marlin are taken from around the 40-fathom curve. At other times, a successful billfisherman has to troll over 100 fathoms of blue water. Not always is the productive water so deep, however.

"A lot of bills come from 28 fathoms near a ledge," says Captain Don Aldridge. "There, about 50 miles out, we have what we call a steeple. It's actually a limestone formation that has been eroded away, and now there are just pillars at about 270 feet of water eroded by the Gulf Stream."

Captain Aldridge of the 48-foot charter boat, "Sea Bea," generally knows where the Gulf Stream can be found and also the location of the best billfishing off Daytona Beach. He has been fishing the area since 1972.

"The 28-fathom curve which runs due east about 45 miles offshore is another good billfish area," he says. "We can set out at the edges of the Gulf Stream and start fishing there. The Gulf Stream location will fluctuate some however."

"May is the beginning of our billfish season, and they will stay here until about November," says the Captain. "We have a lot of sailfish, some marlin, and occasionally, a few whites are caught."

Summer is a good time to chase billfish far offshore in this region.

In the summer months of June, July and August, dolphin move in toward shore and the billfish follow suit. Marlin can then be found as close as 17 miles, and sailfish will come to within nine miles, according to the captain. One summer, a 300-pound blue marlin was taken about 18 miles off the beach.

"During that period, you get the easterly breeze that blows the fresh water closer to the beach," explains Aldridge. "The water will get to 82 or 83 degrees on the beach and the warm water attracts dolphin. The marlin and sailfish aren't far behind."

Blue marlin have been caught as early as February in shallower water, but normally, they're not that thick "in close." By November, they have moved to extremely deep water, according to Aldridge.

"How far out do we normally have to travel to get in on the good billfishing? About 40 miles," says the captain. "Find good blue water and a good temperature like 80.6 degrees and that's where we'll get the strikes. I'll stay once I locate that temperature."

Lots of the sailfish action off Daytona takes place around approximately 30 different natural reefs and several wrecks.

"Some of the wrecks are torpedoed ships dating back to World War II," says the captain. "They all hold a lot of fish. They have also sunk a few barges and Liberty ships off the Daytona area. About six months to a year later, they start attracting some real good fish."

The largest marlin to be hauled on board the "Sea Bea" weighed about 250 pounds, but there are much bigger ones off Daytona Beach. When the big ones come through, several weighing in the range of 500 to 600 pounds are hooked, but many get away.

"You really need to know what you're doing to put a fish like that in the boat," notes the captain. "With charter boats, we get all kinds of anglers -- not always the experienced ones."

Big Events & Facilities

The big fishing event of the year, The Greater Daytona Beach Striking Fish Tournament, becomes more popular each year. Anglers from as far away as North Carolina and Miami fish the event which attracts almost 50 percent of its contestants from outside the Volusia County area. The tournament, limited to the first 200 entries, fills up quickly. Yet, as many as 800 to 1,000 anglers enter because of the huge number of fish caught off Daytona in May.

Marlin, like the 508 pounder taken in 1985 or the tournament record caught in 1986 weighing 582 pounds, are strong attractions. The sailfish record of 67 pounds is more justification for being there. White marlin are rare, and the tournament record is only 52 pounds, 8 ounces, but that's one mark everyone can shoot for.

Visiting anglers won't lack for fine food or places to stay. The Sun Viking Lodge on South Atlantic Avenue and the Clarendon Plaza on North Atlantic Avenue are two particularly fine properties. Favorite restaurants include Aunt Catfish in South Daytona, Down The Hatch and the Inlet Harbor Restaurant at Ponce Inlet. For information on offshore charters or tournaments, contact the Halifax Sport Fishing Club at P.O. Box 4221, South Daytona, FL 32021.

17

INLAND SPRINGS AND CAVE DIVING

Tim demonstrates that fresh water springs are just as lively as the living seas.

This book wouldn't be complete if we didn't mention the numerous clear freshwater springs in both North and Central Florida that attract divers from all over the Eastern U.S.

Spring diving--not to be confused with cave diving--doesn't require any special skill, strength, or daring. Snorkeling or diving in open, sand-bottom spring areas is an activity all family members can enjoy, regardless of expertise. In fact, spring diving is so safe that many dive stores schedule their open-water training dives in many of the springs.

Outside of a pool, there is no safer or better place to swim: clear water, shallow depths of 15-30 feet, no waves to fight, no animals of any kind to fear. Besides the always perfect conditions, the cost factor is probably almost as equally attractive. Many springs are in state parks or near private campgrounds, so divers can choose to sleep in a tent to ensure a very economical dive vacation.

If you've never snorkeled before, the springs are the place to try. I've been a snorkeler longer than I can remember. My parents claim I started exploring the bottom of bath tubs when I was an infant. I don't doubt it since curiosity about aquatic life seems almost instinctive. Give a mask and snorkel to any young child and he'll sightsee in the shallows for hours. It seems to matter little how much he sees or how far he explores. The ability to conquer another world and remain freely in this new habitat is reward enough.

Besides sightseeing and fish watching, the activities for springs snorkelers and divers are varied. You can treasure hunt for lost rings and other jewelry, prehistoric shark teeth, or Indian artifacts.

Or you can develop into the ultimate collector of underwater memorabilia: a photographer. The springs are shallow and clear enough and so well populated with fish life it's worth the several hundred dollar investment needed to take underwater pictures.

Some Florida springs have gained something of an unsavory reputation because of the occasional drowning of divers. However, these deaths take place not in the open water areas of the springs but far underground, in the water-filled limestone tunnels that penetrate deep into the earth.

Although many people equate them, spring diving and cave diving are not the same thing. Cave diving definitely IS dangerous. Cave diving requires advanced knowledge and special equipment that is never covered adequately in any general scuba course. Entering a cave without the proper training is asking for trouble.

But just because caves are dangerous doesn't mean you can't see the insides of a spring. Or their large caverns, huge rock rooms where you can always see the daylight entrance but still require a light to explore fully. A moderate penetration of no more than 25 yards into a cavern (a point where the entrance if often easily visible) is known as a ledge dive.

Experts consider ledge diving a safe activity for any certified scuba diver. Penetrations beyond 25 yards, or any penetration where sight of the entrance is lost, is considered an advanced ledge dive; such a dive not only demands a light but also deployment of a safety line to make finding the way out a safe, sure thing.

If the idea of even ledge diving makes you uncomfortable--if you're one of those who doesn't like having anything over your head but water, which is easy to surface through anytime, any where-- don't feel like you're missing a great deal by staying out of them. Caverns, like caves, tend to be barren places. All the fish life and plants live outside in the bright sunshine. In fact, it's rare that fish enter either caverns or caves--which perhaps ought to tell us all something.

142

The springs are shallow and clear enough and so well populated with fish life it's worth the several hundred dollar investment needed to take underwater pictures.

Florida Springs

Florida boasts 17 of the 75 first-magnitude springs in the U.S., flowing at rates of 100 cubic feet or more per second. There are also 49 second-magnitude springs and countless lesser ones. Which accounts for all the canoes and inner tubes piled on car roofs.

Deliberately missing from this chapter are springs that require divers to take more risk than I care to suggest. If a particular description states that only certified cave divers should go beyond a certain point in a cavern or tunnel, please follow that advice. Dumb divers die in Florida caves every year because they push their limits. Unlike the ocean, there is no fast exit to the surface should you run into trouble deep inside a cave tunnel: only the same way you came in.

● BLUE GROTTO: (from Williston, take U.S.-27A for 2 miles west toward Chiefland. The sign is at a dirt road on the left across from a Catholic Church.) Blue Grotto is an old dive site which was accessible on a sporadic basis until 1988 when new owners turned it into a commercial site open year-round with dive store and air fills. The cavern dive is one of Florida's best. Water temperatures are 72-degrees year-round. Two underwater platforms are offered at 30 feet so divers will stay off the silty bottom; a fresh air bell is at 30 feet. A permanent guideline leads into the cavern, which lacks any sort of dangerous tunnel maze. The bream here love to be fed. Blue Grotto is not affected by rising river waters but may adopt a green tinge during periods of heavy rain. On its best days, Blue Grotto claims 200-foot visibility; 904/528-5770.

● CRYSTAL RIVER: Near the town of Crystal River off U.S. 19. Located on the Gulf Coast just above Homosassa, Crystal River is considered to have the best fresh water fish viewing in the U.S. It is also the only place you can be guaranteed of swimming face to face with the endangered manatee.

From December to March, Crystal River probably has as many fish packed into it as some of the finest saltwater reefs. But what makes it so unique is that the fish are both salt and fresh water species. The main boil, known as King's Spring, is the most crowded. Less crowded spots include Idiot's Delight and Gator Hole on the east side of King's Bay in a canal system. Catfish Corner on the north side of the bay is filled with, guess what. Mullet's Gullet is another good spot. You can get the exact locations to all the sites from any of the boat rental/dive shop operations such as Port Paradise 904/795-3111; Crystal Lodge Dive Center, 904/795-3171 and Plantation inn, 904/795-5797.

● RAINBOW RIVER: Near Dunellon. This clear-water river runs 5-1/2 miles before emptying into the Withlacoochee. The head spring is a failed tourist attraction and closed to land visitors. But it is only 1-1/4 miles upriver from the nearest boat launch. Depths are shallow, only 7-30 feet. Superb setting for underwater photography. Float with the current back to the boat ramp, using either snorkel or scuba. Good relic hunting, and depths are only 10-20 feet. There is talk of closing the river to motorized boat traffic.

● ALEXANDER SPRINGS: (take U.S. 441 to its intersection with St. Rd. 19 at Eustis. Turn right at the overpass and follow St. Rd. 19 for about 15 miles to St. Rd 445. Turn right and follow the signs to the springs, in the Ocala National Forest.) The Alexander Springs spring basin can hold a platoon of snorkelers and divers, which it often does on weekends when training classes are held. However, there is always enough empty water even around the cave, located 27 feet down.

One of the state's larger spring basins, the foliage-lined bank is home to numerous largemouth bass and panfish. Don't be surprised to see ocean-going mullet swimming about, too; they enter via the 15-mile long spring run that empties into the St. Johns which, in turn, empties into the Atlantic. I like the grassy shoreline to the right of the beach entry. You can always find lots of bream to feed, but they are more cooperative if you're wearing scuba instead of snorkeling. The fish don't like to be too close to the surface, where they might be picked off by an otter or gator. I've seen both in this spot. The quick-moving otter--suddenly there one minute, vanished in a flurry of bubbles the next--was the bigger shock.

Alexander Springs offers picnicking, canoe rentals and camping. It's an excellent week-end getaway. However, you may find it a long walk with a tank from

144

Crystal River is an incredible dive spot, home of many fish and manatees.

the parking lot to the water, a distance of several hundred yards. Consider using a luggage cart or wearing it.

● JUNIPER SPRINGS: (located about 5 miles west of the SR-19/SR-40 intersection on SR-40, in the Ocala National Forest). Juniper Springs is one of the oldest national forest recreation areas on the entire eastern seaboard. The spring basin is not as good for snorkeling as the one at nearby Alexander Springs, although the shoreline is more lush and tropical looking. You will find good snorkeling in the spring run, though on weekends especially you'll be forced to share it with canoeists. Juniper contains the same general recreational facilities as Alexander Springs, including campgrounds and canoe rentals.

● SALT SPRINGS:(another commercial campground in the Ocala Forest, it is located on SR-19 in the town of Salt Springs.) You have three spring boils to snorkel around here. The spring basin is good for exploring the caves and crevices, and from there you have a five-mile run which also leads to Lake George. The run is often filled with fish and blue crabs and, on weekends, bass anglers. This is another excellent site for underwater photography because of the large concentrations of largemouth bass and bream. You may see bass as large as 8-12 pounds! I have taken underwater bass photos for every major outdoors magazine in the country in this one spot. However, the area has become so popular, it's quite crowded weekends and holidays.

A word of particular warning here: not long ago a snorkeler was "harassed" by an alligator. The diver came through with a torn wet suit (if the gator had been serious, the bite would have been far worse). Wildlife authorities killed the gator to prevent a repeat attack. Gators can be curious and they are not afraid of people. The only time they are likely to bother anyone is during the mating season. Still, I usually leave the water when I see an alligator here or anywhere. That's why there are only two types of divers: "bold divers" and " old divers." A "bold/old diver" is a rare hybrid, indeed.

● SILVER GLEN SPRINGS: (located off St. Rd. 19 about 6 miles north of the SR-19/SR-40 intersection in the Ocala National Forest.) Snorkeling only is permitted in the large spring basin created by two springs. Striped bass in late summer/early fall often school over the larger spring in 28 feet of water. The most interesting aspect is the deep blue round opening in the sand just below the surface of the smaller spring, which is 6 feet across. You can free dive from the surface into a large room that plunges as much as 42-feet deep. In addition, a half-mile spring run leading to Lake George, part of the St. Johns chain. This tends to be crowded with boat traffic and should not be attempted unless you are beside a canoe or boat of your own. Canoe rentals and camping are available at Silver Glen; 904/685-2514.

● BLUE SPRING/ORANGE CITY: (another 'blue spring,' but this is one of the finest in the Florida state park system; take U.S. 17/92 to Orange City and turn at the stoplight at West French Ave. Park signs will lead you the rest of the way.) The spring boil is huge and issues 121 million gallons of water a day. You can snorkel in the area around the spring as well as snorkel the half-mile long run, which empties into the St. Johns.

Lots of fish throughout the year, including largemouth bass, catfish, gar and tilapia. Fossil shells and shark teeth have also been found. During cold months, the endangered manatee or sea cow uses the springs waters as a refuge against pneumonia, and all diving and snorkeling in the run is prohibited at that time. Sometimes the manatees will go as far as the spring boil, but divers are usually made to leave if they do. Regardless, you can observe them from the observation platform overlooking the spring run. This is known as one of Florida's deadliest springs because divers have insisted on entering the fast-flowing cave shaft. Located in only 10 feet of water, it angles off at a sharp 45-degree angle at 60 feet. The flow is strong enough to knock off masks or dislodge regulators of unwary divers. Only 40 divers at a time are allowed in; arrival must be before 3 p.m. A full tank, light and knife are mandatory. The camping (tent or RV) is excellent; 904/775-3663.

● DE LEON SPRINGS: (go 9 miles north of Deland on U.S. 17)) Once a privately-owned recreation area, De Leon Springs is now a state park. The spring area (170-feet across) has been turned into a swimming pool: the edges are shallow and sandy and a favorite training ground for new scuba divers. The spring reaches 20 feet at its deepest but can be dirty when scuba divers enter the cave and stir up the bottom silt, which comes gushing out of the narrow cave mouth like garbage. The basin is known for its fossil and Indian remains and tales of Spanish treasure

The most popular activity at many fresh water springs is fish feeding.

supposedly left here. No trace of it has ever been located. Scuba is severely restricted, so snorkeling may be your only option. However, the restaurant here is renowned for its make-your-own-pancakes on a hot griddle embedded in your table. That is reason enough to visit: bulk up on some hotcakes and then enter the cool spring water, well fortified.

● ROCK SPRINGS: (just north of Orlando in Apopka's Kelly Park; take SR-435 north from Apopka, and turn right at the dead end at the Bay Ridge/Rock Springs Rd. Rock Springs is only about 1/2-mile from this intersection.) The spring flows from a cave located at the base of a limestone cliff. Past fatalities here have resulted in a grating being put in place to keep swimmers from entering the partially air-filled cave.

● VORTEX SPRING (near the town of Ponce de Leon, just north of I-10's Exit 15): With a maximum depth of 50 feet and a head pool extending 200 feet across, this is a popular spot for instruction and check-out dives. Besides offering a good ledge dive, there's also a cave going back 700 feet, but a locked grate ensures that access is available only to certified cave divers. Vortex Spring is a commercial operation with a modest access fee. Overnight accommodations include campgrounds, dormitories and efficiency rooms. The spring pool is home to at least 18 different species of fish, including huge hybrid Japanese goldfish. A fully stocked dive shop with air fills available. Usually affected by rain runoff for only a day or two: 904/836-4979.

● MORRISON SPRING (also near the town of Ponce de Leon, just south of I-10's Exit 15): One of the best spring dives in the state. Moss-draped cypress trees border the large basin. Two small caves, one at 30 feet and another at 50 feet, offer an excellent introduction to ledge diving; you can never go so far that you lose the sunlight. Another commercial site with entrance fee, air, and rentals. The spring run travels 1/2-mile into the Choctawhatchee River.

● CYPRESS SPRING: (seven miles south of I-10's Exit 17 near the town of Vernon). Another commercial operation allowing both snorkeling and scuba, the basin is 150-feet wide. It's only 25 feet deep to the narrow 6x10 cavern opening, which leads into a room 15 feet high and about 40 feet wide. The back of the room descends to 70 foot depths, but you can always see the light at the opening. Camping, canoes and a concession stand; 904/535-2960

● MERRIT'S MILL POND/BLUE SPRINGS: Located near Marianna, the main spring is known as Blue Springs. As you'll see, the term "blue" crops up frequently in spring names; not surprising considering the color of the water in the deeper springs. This is a prime area offering lots of different snorkeling and scuba opportunities along the spring run, over 5 miles long. Snorkeling only is permitted in the head pool, while scuba is an option virtually everywhere else. Rent a canoe and stop at Twin Caves, Shangri La Spring, Indian Washtub, Gator Spring (not only might you see a gator but also turtles).

● FLORIDA CAVERNS STATE PARK. (3 miles north of Marianna on SR-167.) Both snorkeling and scuba are permitted in the large spring area, known as the Blue Hole. It flows into the Chipola River. Scuba divers need to check in with park personnel before entering the spring.

● WAKULLA SPRINGS (take SR-61 and go 14 miles south of Tallahassee): Not one of the best places for snorkeling, since it is confined to a roped off area and 'gators are definitely a danger.

● WACISSA RIVER SPRINGS (Exit 32 off I-10 near Tallahassee, go 10-1/2 miles on SR-59 to reach the spring): More than a half-dozen different springs form the headwaters of the river, and each can be visited by small boat or canoe. Besides good relic hunting, the Wacissa joins the Aucilla River to create a 14-mile long canoe run.

● LITTLE/BIG DISMAL SINKS: (From Tallahassee, go 9 miles south on SR-319. Take the first dirt road on your right, winding right at the first fork and left at the second.) Inside the Apalachicola National Forest, the park service built platforms for divers, who are admitted from November until March. The northwest wall of Little Dismal has a cave that runs no deeper than 60 feet but penetrates back almost 400-feet. Big dismal has an overhang on the north wall at 85 feet that can be penetrated about 100 feet.

● PARADISE SPRINGS: (coming from the south, take Exit 67 off I-75 onto SR-484 and go east 7 miles to U.S. 441. Turn left onto 441 and go 5 miles to where the median begins. Just 50 feet before the split is a black mailbox with a diver's flag on a dirt road to the right. Follow the dirt road 1/2-mile to the springs.) A new commercial operation at what formerly was called Archway Sink. The spring pool is quite small, only 20-feet across. Two caverns, but the main one of the south is 60-feet wide. The passageway narrows eventually forming a tunnel that goes to 140 feet. Along this passageway, you'll see hundreds of sand dollars, sea biscuits and unidentified bone fragments embedded in the ceilings and walls. An incredible reminder of the prehistoric, sunken Florida of 10,000 years ago. Advance reservations are mandatory: 904/368-5746.

● ICHETUCKNEE SPRINGS: (Exit I-75 at SR-47 and go south for 12 miles on SR-47 to SR-238. Turn right onto SR-238 and follow road to park entrance.) Now part of the state park system, several springs form the Ichetucknee River system. An extremely popular spot for snorkelers, nature lovers and those who like to watch the world go by from an innertube. A wet suit is necessary since once you begin to snorkel or float, there's no turning back against the current; a tram transports you back to your starting point. The float is divided into a northern section (1.4 miles) and a southern section (1.7 miles). Arrive early on summer weekends or you may not get in. Blue Hole Spring, located inside the park, is restricted to certified cave divers because of its strong water flow, difficult to swim against.

● GINNIE SPRINGS: (From US 41, go west onto SR-340 for just over 6-1/2 miles to a graded road on the right with the Ginnie Springs sign.) Ginnie is a large recreational area providing camping, air station and restrooms along with its complex of several springs located here on the banks of the Santa Fe River. Ginnie Springs has a sand bottom loaded with eel grass with a cavern that widens into two separate rooms. Two tunnels have been blocked off with iron grating because of the fatalities in the tunnels. The cavern is rated as an advanced ledge dive. The Devil's Eye spring is one of three outlets found in the same cove with a cypress deck descending to the waterline. The almost perfectly round entrance, at only 6 feet, makes a vertical descent to the 20-foot bottom and the "Devil's Dungeon," a 30x20 foot room on the north side of the shaft. No one but certified cave divers should go beyond this room. The Devil's Ear is at the edge of the Santa Fe. Little Devil is located up the run from the Devil's Eye an excellent photo opportunity. Admission fee; campgrounds available. Call 800/874-8571 or 904/454-2202.

● BLUE SPRINGS/SANTA FE RIVER (situated near High Springs, take US 41 to SR-340 for 4-1/2 miles to the entrance sign): Another commercial operation with camping but permitting snorkeling only. Lots of tame bream that like to be fed, also lots of good plant life. Just east is Naked Springs, where supposedly in times past people too poor to own bathing suits swam naked; sounds like just another excuse for good old-fashioned skinny dipping.

● SANTA FE RIVER: One of the best places in Florida for artifact collecting when rain is scarce and the river drops. Several springs--Big Awesome, Little Awesome, Trackone Siphon and Myrtle's Fissure--line the Santa Fe from Ginnie Springs to SR-47. Fossils and Indian artifacts are commonly found on the bottom along this route. Be sure and display the diver's flag on an inner tube or your canoe if you decide to make this float, a distance of about 2 miles. Consider a wet suit a necessity.

● PEACOCK SPRINGS STATE PARK: (go north on SR-51 from Mayo, turn right on paved road across from the service station in Luraville; go another 2 miles and turn right into the park.) Known previously as Peacock Slough, diving is severely limited if you don't have cavern or cave diving certification since park officials won't let you dive with a light unless you have proper certification.

● CONVICT SPRING/JIM HOLLIS RIVER RENDEZVOUS: (take U.S.-27 from Branford going east or from Mayo headed west; turn at CR-354, Convict Spring Rd. where a large Jim Hollis River Rendezvous sign points the way.) Another commercially operated spring site, the basin is only 50-feet across with depths to 25 feet. A cave that extends back 80 feet reaches a depth of only 30 feet, making this a very safe site. However, this operation run by Jim Hollis of Orlando is the ultimate in Florida fresh water diving luxury. Motel/lodge facilities, restaurant and a beer emporium with 300 different kinds of beer, hot tubs, sauna, pistol and rifle range and canoe rentals make this the ultimate spring diving resort. A pontoon boat makes regular trips to Troy Springs. A shuttle bus provides diver transport to the nearby Peacock spring system. Arrangements can also be made to dive the lower Ichetucknee River. Three-day certification courses also offered. What more can there be? With all the attractions and toys, this is a diver's Disney World. Call 904/294-2510 or 800/533-5276; fax 904/294-1133.

● TROY SPRINGS: (located near Branford, land access has been closed off but can still be reached via the Suwannee River as long as you stay anchored in the basin and don't land on the private property.) This popular spring, lacking any dangerous cave and enjoying depths up to 80 feet, was long a popular check-out dive site. At the end of the spring run are the remains of the old steamboat "Madison" which has rested here since 1863.

● LITTLE RIVER SPRING: (from Branford, go north on U.S.-129 for about 3 miles, then turn left at the Camp 'O the Suwannee sign; bear left at the second sign, over 1-1/2 miles distant.) Considered one of the state's best cave dives, it is restricted to certified cave divers only.

● OTTER SPRINGS: (from Fanning Springs on U.S. 19/98, take SR-26 north to Wilcox, then CR-232 to the RV park). One of the few RV parks to offer scuba diving, the snorkeling opportunities are usually good. A cave at 25 feet is used by the on-site dive shop to teach cave and cavern diving, but it silts up easily if you're not careful. Camping facilities are first-rate.

● MANATEE SPRINGS: (near Chiefland, take U.S-19 to SR-320 and follow the signs to the state park). Named for the sea cows which formerly wintered here, few manatees visit anymore. Park personnel strictly enforce certain regulations: no cave diving certification, no underwater lights. No certification, no diving. If you want to see manatees, go to Crystal River.

18

PANHANDLE ANGLING RECORDS

The Upper Gulf Coast offers numerous world record opportunities, according to Larry.

No other area of the state has the variety and number of world records that the waters off the panhandle possesses. Some of the fishing can be found just a cast-length off the beach while other opportunities are available after an all-day boat ride to the "seemingly center" of the Gulf.

Off the Panhandle, marlin are plentiful, and July is the traditional beginning of the summer season. Big game trollers are exploring the Spur, Nipple and Desoto Canyon, all popular billfishing spots in the area. Numerous tournaments add to the boat activity and results.

Wahoo and yellowfin tuna are other possible catches in the same blue-water areas out in the Gulf. Trolling the blue water and the current eddies is usually the most productive ploy. Rips are located closer to the beach and tuna and other big game fish also move in. That's also where you may find some dolphin all along the Panhandle. Look also for weedlines about 20 to 30 miles out; they attract both dolphin and wahoo.

A long run is still required to reach billfish in the Gulf. Some boats run 50 to 100 miles out to take advantage of the relatively untapped source of white and blue marlin and yellowfin tuna. White marlin are found in the late fall, often in great numbers.

151

Calendar - Panhandle and Upper Gulf Coasts

SPRING	SUMMER	FALL	WINTER
Amberjack	Amberjack	Amberjack	Sea Trout
Barracuda	Marlin	Marlin	Spanish Mackerel
Cobia	Bonito	Sailfish	Grouper
Bluefish	Sailfish	Dolphin	Snapper
King Mackerel	Dolphin	Barracuda	Sea Trout
Pompano	King Mackerel	Redfish	Drum
Sea Trout	Tarpon	Sheepshead	Bluefish
Sheepshead	Cobia	Redfish	
Red Snapper	Sea Trout	Grouper	
Grouper	Spanish Mackerel	Snapper	
Redfish	Grouper	Cobia	
	Snapper	Flounder	

Summer is a good time to chase sailfish far offshore in this region. In the fall, sails move closer to shore and remain there until cool water forces them to follow the current south.

Party boats usually catch grouper and red snapper from their favorite "snapper bank," offshore reef areas that stretch between Pensacola and Panama City. A particularly good bottom fishing spot is a large area of sand and rock ledges located about 25 miles south of Destin. A variety of snapper are taken there in 200 to 250 feet of water. The so-called "240 foot curve" attracts most of the spring-time anglers after red snapper, grouper or scamp.

Another good grouper area of scattered rock and shell is located about 10 miles south of Carrabelle. Grouper fishing in the summer months is often good over any offshore rock pile. One such place with numerous rocky ridges is located about 24 miles southeast of Steinhatchee in 32 to 50 feet of water. A place called, "3 to 5 Ridge" is a sand and rock ledge area in 110 to 150 feet. The ledges are three to five fathoms (18 to 30 feet) tall, and provide excellent habitat for red snapper and Warsaw grouper. To find it, go about 20 miles offshore between Destin and Panama City.

Marker buoys are effective fish attractors off the Northern Gulf Coast.

Off Panama City is a popular red snapper area of flat and hard sand called the "Spawning Grounds." Another spot is located about 15 miles south of Destin in 130 to 185 feet of water. There are 10-foot ledges in the area and a few airplane wrecks scattered about. Another prime are is the "Mud Banks," located about 40 miles off Panama City in 180 to 200 feet of water. The eight-mile long rock ledge is sometimes 20 feet tall in places.

August is the best month for catching red snapper off the panhandle coast. Bottom fishing charters are available out of most ports in the region. In the winter, they run on weekends primarily, for those hardy souls who have to go fishing.

Inshore and Bay Fishing

Speckled trout fishing is very good early and late over grass flats around Perdido Key in the Panhandle. The largest trout often run the pass at the western end of Perdido Key and are caught on an outgoing tide. An option is to fish a deep hole beneath a Panhandle bridge with a live pinfish. Trout and reds are the normal fare, even after dark. Plastic-tailed jigs work particularly well at night.

The trout, redfish and flounder can be found all along the Panhandle in the deeper, warmer waters during the winter months. They frequent the deeper lagoons and bayous, but be warned, the north winds can blow a lot of water out of those places. Tides during the winter may be one and one-half foot lower than the tides of summer.

During the summer, they are in the grass flats. A prime location for large redfish is often Bob Sikes Cut through St. George Island. Live shrimp, hooked just under the "horn", and cast alongside jetties lining the entrances to Gulf passes are usually productive for all three species. A light spinning outfit with small sinker or split shot and a small treble hook are all that's needed to catch some reds and trout.

Early morning flounder fishing trips with cooperating high tides are often successful at the stump hole on Cape San Blas and some of the Panhandle piers. Pier walkers "slow troll" the pilings, pausing at each post. Minnows are effective fished back under the piers also. Whiting are often in the surf during the cooler months. Surf casting from the finger jetties, sandy shores and the 3,000-foot Destin Bridge Catwalk can result in whiting, as well as trout and pompano. The 1,200-foot Okaloosa Pier is lighted for night fishing and is known to shelter big tarpon.

Rivers and Creeks

Redfish, trout, mangrove snapper and sheepshead migrate to the moving water in the fall. The later are often found around the rock jetties and passes in the cold months. Fishing in Gulf waters is very dependent on weather during the winter months. If you are venturing offshore, you definitely need to keep an eye on it. One way, though, to enjoy the fishing of the Gulf of Mexico is in its tributary rivers and creeks.

Fishing from a houseboat around the mouth of the Suwannee River is almost always productive. Miller's Marina at the town of Suwannee rents 44-foot houseboats, and the redfish are a chief attraction to the hoards of anglers that flock to the river mouth. A weekend houseboating vacation provides inshore anglers with the

A particularly good bottom fishing spot is a large area of sand and rock ledges located about 25 miles south of Destin.

freedom to pause and fish any of the cuts or passes around the island-dotted Suwannee mouth and anchor anywhere.

You can take advantage of the late afternoon, night and early morning fishing without having to find your way in the dark. The redfish that pile into the river when the brutal cold hits are voracious feeders after dark. East Pass is renown not only for its redfish, but also for sea trout, flounder and drum fishing. A variety of brackish water species are numerous around the many islands near the Gulf, in the canal systems and in the tributaries feeding the delta.

A peaceful environment of scenic marshes, lagoons and creeks surround the Suwannee watershed near its mouth. There are plenty of places that one can fish brackish water from the houseboat. The fishing, serenity and tranquility around the mouth of the majestic Suwannee River from the comforts of a houseboat cannot be duplicated. For more information, contact Bill Miller, Suwannee

155

Houseboats, P.O. Box 280, Suwannee, FL 32692, or phone (904) 542-7349.

In the rivers and creeks of Florida's northwest coast, sheepshead and trout are usually around in the winter. A particularly productive spot is Spring Creek, which is located in Oyster Bay about 25 miles south of Tallahassee. The mouths of other panhandle rivers also attract the two dependable species. Another hot spot in the winter is the St. Marks River mouth.

On The Move For Variety

Deep jigging for amberjack along the Gulf off the Panhandle is very productive in the summer months. Fishing for large amberjack is best from Cape San Blas to Perdido Key. Tarpon can be in the bays and inshore waters in the summer months. Large 15-pound bluefish migrate northward all along Florida's upper Gulf coast. They are often found around the inshore and offshore rocks.

Cobia migrate along the northwest Gulf coast in March and are taken from piers, the surf and from boats. The run is usually at its best in April and May. Cobia take up residence by any offshore post or marker buoy during June. The best method to take a few is to anchor uptide and cast jigs or drift live bait toward the buoy. These schooling fish are often aggressive so have a partner toss to the area of a hooked fish when possible.

Right behind the cobia are Spanish and king mackerel. The mackerel begin showing up in the northwest Gulf coast during April, and the fish are usually caught all along the upper Gulf coast during May. Trollers are usually kept busy with bites from Spanish mackerel. King mackerel are closer in than the billfish and dolphin of the panhandle. The top September spot for mackerel, bluefish and cobia along the northwest Gulf coast is the wreck of the battleship, USS Massachusetts. It lies partially exposed on a sand ridge off Pensacola.

Destin and Ft. Walton Beach are two communities on the Emerald Coast that offer excellent marinas and accommodations. This northern Gulf coast area with 24-miles of sugar-white sands attracts two million visitors annually, and many come to fish. At Destin, the "World's Luckiest Fishing Village," sits the largest sport fishing fleet in Florida. More than 135 vessels offer deep sea,

The Emerald Coast offers numerous full-service marinas and a variety of accommodations.

inshore and bottom fishing charters with half day, full day and overnight packages.

The geographic locale allows the speediest deepwater access on the Gulf. The 100 Fathom curve and offshore shelf both dip straight into Destin's East Pass, offering 100 foot depths within 10 minutes. Offshore trolling is normally considered to start at the 50 fathom curve which is about 27 miles southwest of Destin. Known as the "Billfish Capital of the Gulf," more billfish are reportedly caught here each year than at all other Gulf ports combined.

Offshore, the area boasts of 20 species of edible gamefish, and not far away is the trout, flounder and redfish fishing in Choctawhatchee Bay. All around the bay and bayous are piers, old pilings, wrecks, rocks and other structures that are great habitat for a variety of species.

157

For further information about fishing in the area, contact the Emerald Coast Tourist Development Council. The address is Dept. LL, P.O. Box 609, Ft. Walton Beach, FL 32549-0609 (telephone 800-322-3319). Those fishing the Panama City area will be very pleased with the accommodations at the Bay Point Marriott on the Gulf. Their Bay Point Yacht and Country Club Marina is home of a big billfish tournament each year. It's the largest private yacht marina on the Gulf Coast. Contact them at 100 Delwood Beach Road, Panama City, FL 32407 or phone (904) 234-3307 or (800) 874-7105.

19

EMERALD COAST DIVING

With few natural reefs but lots of artificial ones, Tim rates this as the most undervalued diving in all Florida.

The Panhandle looks and feels like a separate state that just happens to have been added to Florida's boundaries. This region hasn't seen the same kind of massive growth as the southern and central regions, so life here isn't too different from the way it was 50 years ago. Perhaps that's why the area contains Florida's three most-highly ranked beaches: Perdido Key, Grayton Beach State Recreation Area and St. Joseph State Park.

Furthermore, you can walk for mile after mile on deserted, sugary white sand of the Gulf Island National Seashore which surrounds Pensacola at the western-most tip, perfect for shelling and exploring. Or simply prop up a chair at the water's edge and cast out a fishing line.

Moreover, the offshore diving conditions can be just as unexpectedly pleasant. On calm days, the water takes on the characteristic hue of the Caribbean. When seen from the air, the coastline could pass for that of Grand Cayman or parts of the Turks & Caicos, mile after mile of wonderful white sand beach bordered by dark blue water.

Unfortunately, first impressions are often deceiving, and this is one of those cases. Though certainly not as clear as the Caribbean,

Panhandle visibility is often much better than in the more southern sections of Florida's Gulf Coast. It's also better than in many adjoining states, and it's probably fair to say that almost as many out-of-staters dive the Panhandle as Floridians who, given a choice, understandably will migrate to South Florida waters.

The city of Pensacola claims to be older than even St. Augustine, and its has its own 16th century foundations to support its claim. The small resort cities of Fort Walton, Destin and the Beaches of South Walton are three more spots where you can lose yourself among the tall dunes, surf and sea oats. They're a far cry from nearby Panama City and Panama City Beach, whose carnival thrill rides and rousing atmosphere seem like the heyday of Coney Island.

If the quieter shores of Pensacola, Destin and South Walton haven't already spoiled you, retreat to St. George Island State Recreation Area or the St. Marks National Wildlife Refuge and thousands of unspoiled acres of sea oats, dunes, forest and beach.

Down Under

Few Floridians are aware that the Panama City Marine Institute's Artificial Reef Program has created one of the most diverse underwater playgrounds anywhere. What would you like? Towers? Airplanes? Shipwrecks modern and historic? Bridge spans that lead to nowhere?

● Talk about a place being under-appreciated and under-utilized, though that is bound to change shortly! One of the most recently added as well as one of the most dramatic artificial reefs is the 205-foot tug "Chippewa" sunk in 1990. Sitting upright at 96 feet on a white sand bottom, she is completely intact--including deck machinery--and the cabin is only at 50 feet, the deck 70 feet below. (LORAN: 14012.2/46921.0)

● The old Hathaway Bridge that linked Panama City and its beaches was turned into 19 different artificial reefs in 1988. Placed between 2 and 15 miles out with depths ranging from 42 to 125 feet, they are turning into excellent fish attractors for divers and anglers.

Almost a dozen barges have been sunk as artificial reefs, all within the easy range of divers except for one at 92 feet which has more limited bottom time. These are one of the best places to see the variety of fish and other marine life that inhabit this part of Florida.

	BRIDGES/ Loran Locations				
#1	14070.6	46953.1	#11	14003.8	46790.3
#2	14068.8	46949.0	#12	14074.5	46946.3
#3	14002.4	46914.3	#13	13995.2	46923.3
#4	13997.9	46915.8	#14	14037.2	46977.4
#5	14019.3	47031.1	#15	14025.2	47030.3
#6	14020.1	47022.8	#16	14031.8	46977.0
#7	13949.8	46950.0	#17	14112.6	46841.1
#8	13953.8	46955.8	#18	14002.1	46910.2
#9	13955.4	46961.0	#19	14085.4	46974.0
#10	13952.7	46969.6			

● Inside St. Andrews Bay, you will find 5 steel-hulled lifeboats in 25 feet of water with visibility anywhere from 5-15 feet (LORAN: 14101.7/46987.4). A 150-foot tar barge at 18 feet is often used for checkout dives even though visibility is no better here than the lifeboats. Called the "Spanish Shanty Barge" because of its position near Spanish Shanty Cove (LORAN: 14101.4/46985.1)

BARGES/ Loran Locations			
Blown-up Barge	65 feet	14052.4	46992.5
Deep Barge	92 feet	13979.8	46962.9
Smith Barge	70 feet	14066.9	46976.0
PCMI Barge	72 feet	14042.8	46999.8
Inshore Twin	71 feet	14069.0	46968.0
Davis Barge	55 feet	14116.0	46916.4
Holland Barge	65 feet	14065.7	46981.1
Long Beach Barge	50 feet	14067.3	47018.3
Spanish Shanty	18 feet	14101.4	46985.1
Offshore Twin	73 feet	14067.7	46967.0
B & B Barge	42 feet	14087.3	46970.7

● Best dived at high tide because it is so close to shore, the tug "E.E. Simpson" rests in 20 feet of water. You can even see the smokestack underwater. (LORAN: 14121.6/46942.6).

● Nearby is the "LOSS Pontoon," a prototype pontoon at 60 feet and down since 1978. The pontoon is 40 feet long and 15 feet in diameter. (LORAN: 14078.0/46973.7) The 107-foot steel-hulled tug "Chickasaw" rests at 75 feet, also since the late 70s. (LORAN: 14056.8/46978.6)

● The Navy has been kind enough to sink research towers similar in shape to oil rigs to attract marine life. Stage II (LORAN: 14069.3/46997.8) is only 3 miles offshore in 60 feet of water; the tower profile is 35 feet. A Navy T-33 trainer at 60 feet is also located just south of Stage II (LORAN: 14069.4/46997.1) The Stage I tower (LORAN: 13980.2/46957.9) is 13 miles out in 107 feet of water with a profile of better than 60 feet.

● One of the most popular dives is the 184-foot long tender "USS Strength;" its deck is at a shallow 40 feet. It was sunk in 1987 to test some new explosive devices; obviously, they worked. Just 5-1/2 miles from the St. Andrews jetties. (LORAN: 14076.7/46943.9) Out another 2 miles is 441-foot "The Liberty Ship" sunk in 1977 in 72 feet of water. The profile is a modest 20 feet off the bottom since the ship was cut at the waterline, but turtles and even manta rays have been sighted in summer. (LORAN: 14064.9/46918.7)

● The Midway Artificial Reef is 4-1/2 miles from the St. Andrews jetties. The site is 72 feet deep and the bottom is scattered with low profile material. Two boxcars sunk in 1988 have deteriorated rapidly. Worth seeing is a Sikorsky-76 air-rescue helicopter. (LORAN: 14072.6/46949.6)

● Panama City also has small limestone reefs called ledges, which are the remnants of prehistoric sea levels. The Warsaw Hole 9 miles southwest of the St. Andrews jetties is the closest. Horseshoe-shaped and with a profile 5-6 feet high, it has many sponges and octocorals and tropicals. Also good for gamefish which change with the season. LORAN: 14033.8/46969.5)

● A mile farther southwest is the 44-foot long, 30-foot diameter Quonset Hut, another gift from the Navy in 82 feet of water. Grouper and snapper reside in winter, amberjack and barracuda in summer. (LORAN: 14011.1/46966.9)

Panhandle visibility is often much better than in the more southern sections of Florida's Gulf Coast.

● West of the St. Andrews jetties are three shipwrecks, one with a tragic history. At 9 1/2 miles out, the "Tarpon" was a 160-foot coastal freighter that sank in a 1937 storm with 18 of her crewmen. Resting at 92 feet, the stern and bow are partly intact and the smokestack is still present on the deck. Surrounding it are bottles of well-aged beer, the final cargo. (LORAN: 13979.5/47001.7) The wreck of the 65-foot tug the "Commander," intact and upright, is in 96 feet about 15 miles from the jetties. (LORAN: 13968.0/46982.3) Twenty-two miles distant is the 105-foot military tugboat the "Grey Ghost" on her side at 108 feet. (LORAN: 13891.11/46991.7)

● Only a half mile in from the "Tarpon" is the Fontainebleau Artificial Reef, mostly of concrete and steel but also a couple of railroad boxcars and an Air Force drone. (LORAN: 14019.7/47028.5)

Philips Inlet, 13 miles west of Panama City, has an excellent ledge system rising 2-4 feet ranging from 60 to 110 feet. It is well-known for spiny lobster as large as 6-12 pounds. Moving farther east along the Panhandle is the St. Joseph peninsula and St. Joe Bay, long a well-known hangout for fish.

● The most famous site is 20 miles south of Cape San Blas: the wreck of the "Empire Mica," ranked one of Florida's best wreck dives. This 465-foot British tanker was sunk by a German submarine in 1942. Sitting at 110 feet, a deck section is still upright and contains its most famous symbol, an 18-foot wide spare propeller. Visibility is usually quite good, with grouper, cudas, snapper and amberjack often present. (LORAN: 14023.5/46489.6)

● Speaking of Cape San Blas, 14 miles out are the remains of the third brick lighthouse built on this spot. The last one dates from 1859 and is now in 25 feet of water. Although the lighthouse is gone, its light is still functioning on shore in a steel tower. (LORAN: 14113.2/46679.1) Only 8 miles offshore, the Cape San Blas Buoy marks three miles of limestone ledges well-known for its clamming. Five miles west is the 65-foot shrimp boat "Captain Kato" which sank in 1988 in 65 feet of water. Stingrays, grouper and snapper all seem to like this fiberglass vessel, which still has its rigging out.

● Panama City gave Port St. Joe a 165-foot long section of its Hathaway Bridge as a fish attractor. Ten miles out, it profiles 36 feet off the 100-foot bottom. (LORAN: 14003.8/46790.3)

● A couple of barges west of the Port St. Joe sea buoy usually contain quite active fish life. One is 3-1/2 miles out at 70 feet. (LORAN: 14098.1/46840.9) Six miles out are the limited remains of "Bill's Barge" at 80 feet. The main part of the ship has collapsed though the four corners survive which flounder, snapper and grouper favor. (LORAN: 14059.1/46836.8)

● You'll need to check with Capt. Black's Marine in Port St. Joe to discover the location of his privately maintained 70-foot long "Gatewood Barge" at 80 feet. No spearing permitted and the macro photography is said to be superb. For night diving, the 170-foot long "Lumber Ship" just 2 miles out is a favorite. At only 22 feet, its remains are easily accessible. (LORAN: 14142.9/46830.5)

If you have your own boat and charts, you'll locate many other ledge formations along the Panhandle which are not regularly serviced by dive shops. This is a huge, vast area still waiting for greater discovery. Many of these ledges close-in hold grouper, snapper, nurse sharks and a host of other marine life that have yet to see the first diver enter the water.

20

EXPLORING FIRST COAST FISHING

Larry's angling adventures are numerous in this historical region.

My third cast to the "draining" oyster bed was stopped, not by bottom entanglements, but by a three pound trout. I worked it into the boat quickly as Terry LaCoss set the hook from his bow casting platform. We had a double, but when his drag zizzled, we knew that the two fish were different species.

His redfish stirred up the outgoing tidal water in the rapidly-drying flat before Terry could pressure it to the boat. It was a three pounder that, like so many other redfish, thought it was eight. From our anchored positioned we continued to toss Countdown Rapalas to the rocky flat in front of the old docks for the next two hours. About 25 fish later, it was time to go.

The guide and I were fishing in Amelia River near downtown Fernandina Beach around some docks that date back to the 1800's. The area boasts some of the earliest settlements in the U.S., thus, it bills itself as "Florida's First Coast." Given the healthy combination of seatrout, redfish and flounder we caught in a short two hours, it's also a first class, but little-known, inshore angling destination.

Terry, who runs a charter operation at Amelia Island and Fernandina Beach, is more familiar with the area's fishing than any other angler I know. Every time I have fished that northeast area of the state with him, I have caught good numbers of fish.

Calendar - North Atlantic Coast			
SPRING	**SUMMER**	**FALL**	**WINTER**
King Mackerel	Spanish Mackerel	King Mackerel	Sheepshead
Dolphin	Sea Trout	Sea Trout	Sea Trout
Cobia	Cobia	Flounder	Grouper
Pompano	Flounder	Bluefish	Snapper
Sea Trout	Redfish	Drum	
Bluefish	Tarpon	Grouper	
Redfish	Grouper	Snapper	
Mangrove Snapper	Snapper	Tarpon	
Spanish Mackerel	Mangrove Snapper	Mangrove Snapper	
Tarpon	Permit	Redfish	
Grouper	Barracuda		
Snapper			

My friend always has the best spots picked out. Anywhere you find pilings, shellfish and moving water is a good one, according to Terry. When the tide is not moving over the structure or close to it on a dropoff, you need to look for such conditions to be successful.

"There are some holes better than others," he admits. "The deeper holes seem to be better if you have massive amounts of pilings, shells and rocks. But the fish will also bite on sandbars, as you know."

We had been at the foot of the St. Mary's jetties about a mile from the inlet mouth earlier and found that out. We caught four trout quickly from that spot. The trout fishing, though, is good several miles upriver. You can even catch trout and saltwater striper as far as five miles upriver. At some areas east of the I-95 bridge, you can catch stripers, freshwater bass, seatrout, redfish and flounder all in the same spot.

Terry likes catching trout. The trout season is good all year, but if you want a giant like the guide's 11 pounder, you are wise to fish the area from March through May. That's when you can catch the big roe trout. An average "gator" trout will weigh six pounds. An angler can only keep one trout over 24 inches (according to existing laws) and the rest of the limit must be between 14 and 24 inches.

The trout season is good all year in Northeast Florida, according to guide Terry LaCoss.

"That 11-pounder struck a Shad Rap in late November," says Terry. "The tide was barely going out, and I switched to a deepwater pattern and cast to five or six foot or water. At eight to ten foot, you'll usually find the dropoff. It is like a sheer cliff with a lot of pilings nearby."

For sheer numbers of trout, Terry recommends the fall action from October through December. A lot of schooling trout in the inlets of the rivers then will average two pounds, according to the guide. You also have a chance to catch them up to 10 pounds in the spring.

Intracoastal Tactics

Moving water is vital to catching trout in the Matanzas River and other intracoastal waters of Northeast Florida. So is matching the forage. When trout are feeding on finger mullet, Rapalas work well in the river. Anytime you're fishing in the intracoastal river or the jetties at Fernandina, Jacksonville, or St. Augustine, you need

167

to imitate the bait that the fish are feeding on. If you're fishing on the jetties, a shrimp imitation grub is most effective.

On shallow shell beds in the flats along the rivers, use a floating jerkbait and float it over the beds. As the tide drops and the current moves away from the jetty, you may want to use a deep running crankbait. When tide comes back in, use a floating minnow bait or other floating lure.

Flats fishing on the Northeast rivers and creeks are best during overcast days. On very warm days or very bright days, the trout normally stay in deeper water and won't come up on the structure. Under those conditions, fishing the low-light times early and late is better.

"Just before a cold front, the trout get very active," says Lacoss, "but after the second day, you will need much smaller line and lures. I may go down to a 2" Rapala and lighter line when fishing the shallow shell beds then."

Most trout and redfish in the intracoastal like a slow retrieve over structure. If you keep the lure in the strike zone as much as possible, you'll catch fish. If you get hung up, shake the rod tip softly to loosen it. A lot of times a fish will be watching the lure and will hit it when it comes loose.

Live shrimp or liver finger mullet are effective in the shallows. The preferred method is to freeline them without a float. In deep water, a 14 to 18 inch leader, swivel and a one or two ounce sinker will get the bait down to work effectively near the bottom. Another effective presentation over the shallow shell beds is a poppin' cork.

In January and February, the fishing is variable, either very good or very bad, depending on the cold fronts. Success also depends on what the shrimp do. When the water is cold, the shrimp leave the rivers and bury themselves in the mud, or they go out to the ocean. If there's no forage around the shell beds, the fish become dormant. After a warming trend, the fish become active again on the second or third day.

Redfish, Flounder & Mackerel
With the Nassau Sound, Cumberland Sound and the Amelia River nearby, the fishing variety near Amelia Island is significant. Kingfish, tarpon and other deep sea species are abundant, thanks to

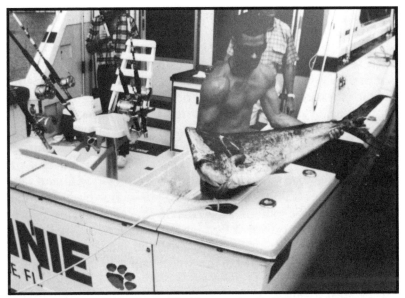

Dolphin catches off Northeast Florida near the Gulf Stream are best during the spring months.

a myriad of bottom ledges, offshore wrecks and the 20 Fathom Curve. Sheepshead and bluefish are often caught from a 1,500-foot pier at Cumberland Sound, and surf casting from finger jetties and sandy shores southward to St. Augustine produces trout, whiting and flounder.

Redfish in Northeast Florida will normally average three to six pounds. Occasionally, an angler will locate and catch a 15 or 20 pounder in the river, but not often. The big redfish are multiplying, and the smaller fish are fun to catch over the shell beds. Big flounder also hang out close to the inlets and the bridges. In fact, a couple of 19-pound records were taken from the Nassau Bridge on the south end of Amelia Island.

The hottest months of the year cause much of the angling success to occur after dark or in the low-light periods of the day. Offshore, blue water species are less affected by the blistering sun than shallower marine life. Swordfishing at night is the norm, and it is particularly worthwhile in the Atlantic off St. Augustine. A

169

surprise catch, slowly becoming more common off the chum lines intended for swordfish, are dolphin or tuna.

May, June and July are the best months for trolling the Gulf Stream about 25 miles off St. Augustine for king mackerel. Most of the really big kings are caught in this region of the state. In fact, fishing for king mackerel is so hot off this coast that numerous large tournaments are held annually here focusing on the species.

You can also often find them in abundance at the mouth of the St. Johns River. King and Spanish mackerel are often found around the sea buoy off Mayport in the summer. The bottom here is shell and grass patches with scattered, low rocks in 44 to 58 feet of water.

As is true all along the Atlantic, dolphin action by the weedlines is a lot of fun. Schoolers at the Gulf Stream edge and big bulls and cows further out on debris floating in the blue water are the sport. Where there's dolphin, there's also blue marlin, especially off Jacksonville's coast. Most of the winter fishing for big game species occurs 16 to 25 miles seaward.

Bottom fishing in the Atlantic warms up in the summer months, and one good area to try is located about 20 miles southeast of St. Augustine. The hard shell and sand bottom lies in 110 feet of water and covers about three square miles. Another good area that covers about two miles is located 25 miles southeast of the nation's oldest city. It is a 360-foot peak in water that drops to over 900 feet. A third good snapper and grouper hole in the same direction is the "Long John," a rock ridge cliff in about 80 feet of water.

A good winter-time spot for red snapper and grouper is located about 20 miles offshore between Mayport and St. Augustine in about 120 feet of water. The reef has a rolling, hard sand bottom. Straight east of Mayport about 25 miles is the "East Grounds," a rock and coral reef habitat for bottom fish in 160 to 170 feet of water.

For information on Amelia Island, contact Amelia Island Chamber of Commerce, 102 Centre St., Fernandina Beach, FL 32034, or phone (904) 261-3248. Superb accommodations are available at The Ritz-Carlton, 4750 Amelia Island Parkway, Amelia Island, FL 32034, phone (904) 277-1100, the Amelia Island Plantation, Amelia Island, FL 32034, phone (800) 342-6841, and the Marriott at Sawgrass Resort, 1000 TPC Blvd., Ponte Vedra Beach, FL 32082, phone (904) 285-7777.

21

DIVING NORTHEAST FLORIDA

Tim knows things are a lot fishier around Jacksonville than most divers realize.

Between Daytona and Jacksonville are miles and miles of mostly deserted beach. Following Highway A1A north from Daytona to St. Augustine will take you by the state's oldest marine park, Marineland of Florida. Originally built in the 1930s as an underwater film studio, this is where Florida dolphins first publicly performed.

St. Augustine generally is regarded as the oldest city in the U.S. Already 55 years old when the Pilgrims landed at Plymouth Rock, St. Augustine is still remarkably small with only around 20,000 people. However, the city limits are packed with entertainment and historic sites.

As a large semi-industrial city, Jacksonville has little to offer tourists except shopping, so go where the residents go: to tiny, timeless Amelia Island which is just two miles wide and 13 miles long. Amelia Island's largest village is Fernandina Beach. Over four centuries old, it has a 30-block historic district listed in the National Register of Historic Places.

Fishy Business Galore

The waters around Jacksonville have a far denser fish population than most divers realize. It's the result of happenstance (a fortuitous grouping of limestone ledges) and planning (the implementation of an extensive artificial reef program). Once almost the exclusive

171

realm of spearfishermen, sight-seeing sport divers are finally in the process of discovering just how good diving conditions are.

Weather is an important variable here: summer by far is usually the best, when the water is calmest and the visibility can reach even 100 feet. The depths off Jacksonville, too, are not as extreme as many other Atlantic coast locations. The typical dive to most wrecks and ledges is between 60 and 100 feet. Better yet, the boat runs aren't always as far offshore as at Daytona and Port Canaveral, though some wrecks are quite a distance from the Mayport inlet.

● Amberjack Hole is ranked Jacksonville's prettiest natural reef formation. The ledges average 10 feet and are host to a thick coating of sponges and corals. Depths range from 75-85 feet, visibility of about 40. Big schools of amberjack that frequent here give the reef its name. About 19 miles from Mayport. (LORAN: 45209.9/61849.9)

● As good as Amberjack Hole is, Clayton's Holler probably sees more divers than any other area. The site is composed of three separate ledge systems, each containing about a dozen ledges. Visibility averages 40 feet, depths 85-90 feet. The northernmost ledges (LORAN: 45132.0/61916.1) have an opening near the center large enough for a diver to swim through. The mile long middle reef (LORAN: 45117.3/61914.6) contains two tug boats and a barge nearby. The tallest ledges, as much as 15 feet high, are at the southern section. (LORAN: 45114.2/61923.1) Clayton's Holler is about 17 miles out.

● Montgomery's Reef, only about 9 miles distant, is a grouping of over a dozen shipwrecks notorious for drawing grouper, sheepshead, snapper and amberjack. Natural ledges in the area, which averages 65 feet, contain interesting marine life. (LORAN: 45232.7/61958.9)

● Rabbit's Lair has an outstanding ledge system almost 10 feet high in spots. Added enticements for marine life to hold close by are a wooden tug, barge and mine sweeper. About 13 miles out. (LORAN: 45248.6/61914.1)

● Nine Mile Reef (which is over 10 miles from the Mayport jetties but what the heck) houses a number of popular wreck dives. The "Asphalt Barge," "Vic's Barge, the "Open-sided Barge" along with a 52-foot tug house grouper, sheepshead and flounder. The tug still yields interesting artifacts. (LORAN: 45192.0/61944.8)

Weather is an important variable here. Even in the summer a full wet suit is necessary. Visibility is often best during the hottest months of the year.

● The Middle Ground (LORAN: 45130.6/61937.3) contains a grouping of small natural ledges and a steel tug at 85 feet has a good sponge and octocoral coating. Nearby, the Japanese government paid for an experimental pyramid-shaped reef made up of fiberglass which is working well. (LORAN: 45141.4/61946.1) These sites are about 14 miles offshore.

● The Gator Bowl is named for the old press boxes dumped here in about 85 feet. They and nearby natural reefs draw good schools of spadefish and amberjack. (LORAN: 45149.9/61887.5)

● The 180-foot freighter "Anna" (LORAN: 45128.8/61808.8) was sunk deliberately in 1986 about 23 miles offshore. Although the cargo hold is broken up, the bow and stern are still intact. A small reef area close by known as "lobster Hotel" also houses a tug and barge. (LORAN: 45151.4/61800.0)

● The 150-foot freighter "Hudgins" sunk in 1987 sits upright at 105 feet. Huge clouds of spadefish, amberjack and baitfish are almost always present. A very picturesque location, 25 miles from the Mayport jetties, although best visibility are only around 50 feet. (LORAN: 45077.3/61813.9)

● The LST "Casa Blanca" also attracts big schools of spadefish and amberjack and visibs here 30 miles offshore can attain 100 feet. The ship sits upright at 112 feet, 85 feet to the upper deck. (LORAN: 45012.7/61795.2)

● Blackmar's Reef, over 25 miles out, contains 5 large wrecks and a number of small ledges. Spadefish and amberjack cloud the water near the shipwrecks. Two airplanes, a WWII Corsair and a Banshee jet fighter, also sit upright on the bottom which varies from 95-110 feet. Ships include the "Warwick" (LORAN: 45047.5/61783.7); the "Ocean Going Tug" (LORAN; 45050.7/61788.7); and the "Super Barge" (LORAN: 45050.3/61785.3)

Jacksonville...who would have guessed the diving could be this good?

APPENDICES

FISHING & HUNTING RESOURCE DIRECTORY

If you are interested in more productive fishing and hunting trips, then this info is for you!

Larsen's Outdoor Publishing is the publisher of several quality Outdoor Libraries - all informational-type books that focus on how and where to catch America's most popular sport fish, hunt popular and exciting big game, camp, dive or travel to exotic destinations.

The perfect-bound, soft-cover books include numerous illustrative graphics, line drawings, maps and photographs. The BASS SERIES LIBRARY as well as the HUNTING LIBRARIES are nationwide in scope. The INSHORE SERIES covers coastal areas from Texas to Maryland and foreign waters. The OUTDOOR TRAVEL SERIES and the OUTDOOR ADVENTURE LIBRARY cover the most exciting destinations in the world. The BASS WATERS SERIES focuses on the top lakes and rivers in the nation's most visited largemouth bass fishing state.

All series appeal to outdoorsmen/readers of all skill levels. The unique four-color cover design, interior layout, quality, information content and economical price makes these books hot sellers in the marketplace. Best of all, you can learn to be more successful in your outdoor endeavors!!

THE BASS SERIES LIBRARY

by Larry Larsen

1. FOLLOW THE FORAGE FOR BETTER BASS ANGLING VOL. 1 BASS/PREY RELATIONSHIP
Learn how to determine the dominant forage in a body of water, and you will consistently catch more and larger bass.

2. FOLLOW THE FORAGE FOR BETTER BASS ANGLING VOL. 2 TECHNIQUES
Learn why one lure or bait is more successful than others and how to use each lure under varying conditions.

3. BASS PRO STRATEGIES
Learn from the experience of the pros, how changes in pH, water temperature, color and fluctuations affect bass fishing, and how to adapt to weather and topographical variations.

4. BASS LURES - TRICKS & TECHNIQUES
Learn how to rig or modify your lures and develop specific presentation and retrieve methods to spark or renew the interest of largemouth!

5. SHALLOW WATER BASS
Learn specific productive tactics that you can apply to fishing in marshes, estuaries, reservoirs, lakes, creeks and small ponds. You'll likely triple your results!

6. BASS FISHING FACTS
Learn why and how bass behave during pre- and post-spawn, how they utilize their senses and how they respond to their environment, and you'll increase your bass angling success! This angler's guide to bass lifestyles and behavior is a reference source never before compiled.

7. TROPHY BASS
Take a look at geographical areas and waters that offer better opportunities to catch giant bass, as well as proven methods and tactics for man made/natural waters. "How to" from guides/trophy bass hunters.

8. ANGLER'S GUIDE TO BASS PATTERNS
Catch bass every time out by learning how to develop a productive pattern quickly and effectively. Learn the most effective combination of lures, methods and places for existing bass activity.

9. BASS GUIDE TIPS
Learn the most productive methods of top bass fishing guides in the country and secret techniques known only in a certain region or state that may work in your waters. Special features include shiners, sunfish kites & flies; flippin, pitchin' & dead stickin', rattlin', skippin' & jerk baits; deep, hot and cold waters; fronts, high winds & rain.

INSHORE SERIES
by Frank Sargeant

IL1. THE SNOOK BOOK

"Must" reading for anyone who loves the pursuit of this unique sub-tropic species. Every aspect of how you can find and catch big snook is covered.

IL2. THE REDFISH BOOK

Packed with expertise from the nation's leading redfish anglers and guides, this book covers every aspect of finding and fooling giant reds. You'll learn secret techniques revealed for the first time.

IL3. THE TARPON BOOK

Find and catch the wily "silver king" along the Gulf Coast, north through the mid-Atlantic, and south along Central and South American coastlines. Experts share their most productive techniques.

IL4. THE TROUT BOOK

You'll learn the best seasons, techniques and lures in this comprehensive book. Entertaining, informative reading for both the old salt and rank amateur.

BASS WATERS SERIES

by Larry Larsen

Take the guessing game out of your next bass fishing trip. The most productive bass water are described in this multi-volume series, plus ramp information, seasonal tactics, water characteristics and much more, including numerous maps and drawings and comprehensive index.

BW1. GUIDE TO NORTH FLORIDA BASS WATERS
From Orange Lake north and west.

BW2. GUIDE TO CENTRAL FLORIDA BASS WATERS
From Tampa/Orlando to Palatka.

BW3. GUIDE TO SOUTH FLORIDA BASS WATERS
From I-4 to the Everglades.

DEER HUNTING LIBRARY
by John E. Phillips

DH1. MASTERS' SECRETS OF DEER HUNTING

Increase your deer hunting success significantly by learning from the masters of the sport. New tactics and strategies.

DH2. THE SCIENCE OF DEER HUNTING

Specific ways to study the habits of deer to make your next scouting and hunting trips more successful. Learn the answers to many of the toughest deer hunting problems a sportsman ever encounters.

TURKEY HUNTING LIBRARY
by John E. Phillips

TH1. MASTERS' SECRETS OF TURKEY HUNTING

Masters of the sport have solved some of the most difficult problems you will encounter while hunting wily longbeardswith bows, blackpowder guns and shotguns.

OUTDOOR TRAVEL SERIES
by Timothy O'Keefe and Larry Larsen

Candid guides with vital recommendations that can make your next trip much more enjoyable.

OT1. FISH & DIVE THE CARIBBEAN - Volume 1

Northern Caribbean, including Cozumel, Caymans, Bahamas, Virgin Islands and other popular destinations.

OT3. FISH & DIVE FLORIDA & the Keys

Featuring fresh water springs; coral reefs; barrier islands; Gulf Stream/passes; inshore flats/channels and back country estuaries.

OUTDOOR ADVENTURE LIBRARY
by Vin T. Sparano

OA1. HUNTING DANGEROUS GAME

Know how it feels to face game that hunts back. You won't forget these classic tales of hunting adventures for grizzly, buffalo, lion, leopard, elephant, jaguar, wolves, rhinos and more!

LARSEN'S OUTDOOR PUBLISHING
CONVENIENT ORDER FORM
(All Prices Include Postage & Handling)

BASS SERIES LIBRARY - only $11.95 each - $79.95 autographed set

_____ 1. Better Bass Angling - Vol. 1- Bass/Prey Interaction

_____ 2. Better Bass Angling - Vol. 2 - Techniques

_____ 3. Bass Pro Strategies

_____ 4. Bass Lures - Tricks & Techniques

_____ 5. Shallow Water Bass

_____ 6. Bass Fishing Facts

_____ 7. Trophy Bass

_____ 8. Angler's Guide to Bass Patterns

_____ 9. Bass Guide Tips

> **BIG SAVINGS!**
> Order 1 book, discount 5%
> 2-3 books, discount 10%.
> 4 or more books discount 20%.

INSHORE SERIES - only $11.95 each or $35.95 for autographed set

_____ IL1. The Snook Book   _____ IL3. The Tarpon Book

_____ IL2. The Redfish Book   _____ IL4. The Trout Book

BASS WATERS SERIES - only $14.95 each or $37.95 autographed set

_____ BW1. Guide To North Florida Bass Waters

_____ BW2. Guide To Central Florida Bass Waters

_____ BW3. Guide to South Florida Bass Waters

BOOKS FROM OTHER SERIES- only $11.95 each

_____ DH1. Masters' Secrets of Deer Hunting

_____ DH2. The Science of Deer Hunting

_____ TH1. Masters' Secrets of Turkey Hunting

_____ OA1. Hunting Dangerous Game

OUTDOOR TRAVEL SERIES - only $13.95 each

_____ OT1. Fish & Dive the Caribbean Vol 1 - Northern Caribbean

_____ OT3. Fish & Dive Florida & the Keys

NAME _____

ADDRESS_____

CITY_____STATE_____ZIP_____

No. of books ordered _____ x $_____ each = _____

No. of books ordered _____ x $_____ each = _____

Multi-bookDiscount (%)   = _____

TOTAL ENCLOSED (Check or Money Order) $_____

Copy this page and mail to:
Larsen's Outdoor Publishing, Dept. RD92
2640 Elizabeth Place, Lakeland, FL 33813

Save Money on Your Next Outdoor Book!

Because you've purchased a Larsen's Outdoor Publishing Book, you can be placed on our growing list of **preferred customers.**

- You can receive special discounts on our wide selection of Bass Fishing, Saltwater Fishing, Hunting, Outdoor Travel and other economically-priced books written by **our expert authors.**

PLUS...

- **Receive Substantial Discounts for Multiple Book Purchases! And...advance notices on upcoming books!**

Send in your name TODAY to be added to our mailing list

___ Yes, put my name on your mailing list to receive:

1. Advance notice on **upcoming outdoor books.**
2. Special **discount offers.**

Name_____

Address_____

City/State/Zip_____

**Send to: Larsen's Outdoor Publishing, Special Offers,
2640 Elizabeth Place, Lakeland, FL 33813**

CHAMBERS OF COMMERCE

South Florida

Brevard County
Melbourne Chamber of Commerce
1005 East Strawbridge Ave.
Melbourne, FL 32901
407/724-5400

Broward County
Ft. Lauderdale Chamber of
    Commerce
P.O. Box 14516
Fort Lauderdale, FL 33302
305/462-6000

Charlotte County
Port Charlotte Chamber of
    Commerce
2702 Tamiami Trail
Port Charlotte, FL 33952
813/627-2222

Collier County
Naples Area Chamber of
    Commerce
1700 North Tamiami Trail
Naples, FL 33940
813/262-6141

Dade County
Miami/Dade Convention
    & Visitors Bureau
701 Brickell Ave. #2700
Miami, FL 33131
800/283-2707

Lee County Convention
    & Visitors Bureau
P.O. Box 2445
Fort Myers, FL 33902
800/237-6444

Manatee County
P.O. Box 321
Bradenton, FL 34206
813/748-3411

Monroe County
Florida Keys Visitors Bureau
P.O. Box 866
Key West, FL 33041
800-FLA-KEYS

Palm Beach County
    Convention & Visitors Bureau
1555 Palm Beach Lakes Blvd.
West Palm Beach, FL 33401
407/471-3995

Sarasota County
P.O. Box 30
Sarasota, FL 34230
813/955-8187

St. Lucie County
2200 Virginia Ave.
Fort Pierce, FL 34982
407/461-2700

Central Florida

Citrus County
P.O. Box 1397
Chiefland, FL 32626
904/726-2801

Hernando County
101 East Ft. Dade Ave.
Brooksville, FL 34601
904/796-2420

Hillsborough County/Tampa CVB
111 Madison St. #1010
Tampa, FL 33602
800/826-8358

Indian River County
P.O. Box 2947
Vero Beach, FL 32961
407/567-3491

Lake County
P.O. Box 774
Sorrento, FL 32776
904/383-8801

Marion County
P.O. Box 11206
Ocala, FL 32673
904/347-3434

Orange County (East)
P.O. Box 27027
Orlando, FL 32867
407/277-5951

Orange County (West)
P.O. Box 522
Winter Garden, FL 32787
407/656-1304

Pasco County
407 W. Main St.
New Port Richey, FL 34652
813/842-7651

Pinellas County/Suncoast CVB
4625 East Bay Dr. #109
Clearwater, FL 34624
813/530-6452

Seminole County
P.O. Box 150784
Altamonte Springs, FL 32715
407/834-4404

Sumter County
P.O. Box 550
Bushnell, FL 33513
904/793-3099

North Florida

Alachua County
P.O. Box 387
Alachua, FL 32615
904/462-3333

Bay County
P.O. Box 1850
Panama City, FL 32402
904/785-5206

Bradford County
P.O. Box 576
Starke, FL 32091
904/964-5278

Calhoun County
314 E. Central Ave.
Blountstown, FL 32424
904/674-4519

Clay County
P.O. Box 1441
Orange Park, FL 32067
904/264-2651

Columbia County
P.O.Box 566
Lake City, FL 32056
904/752-3690

Dixie County
P.O. Box 547
Cross City, FL 32628
904/498-3367

Duval County/Jacksonville
P.O. Box 329
Jacksonville, FL 32201
904/353-0300

Escambia County/Pensacola
P.O. Box 550
Pensacola, FL 32593
904/438-4081

Flagler County
2 Airport Rd.
Star Route Box 18-N
Bunnell, FL 32110

Franklin County/Apalachicola Bay
128 Market St.
Apalachicola, FL 32320
904/653-9419

Gilchrist County
P.O. Box 186
Trenton, FL 32693
904/463-6327

Gulf County
P.O. Box 628
Wewahitchka, FL 32465
904/639-2130

Lafayette County
P.O. Box 416
Mayo, FL 32066
904/294-2918

Levy County/Chiefland Area
P.O. Box 1397
Chiefland, FL 32626
904/726-2801

Nassau County/Amelia Island
P.O. Box 472
Fernandina Beach, FL 32034
904/261-3248

Okaloosa County/Crestview
502 S. Main Street
Crestview, FL 32536
904/682-3212

Putnam County
P.O. Box 550
Palatka, FL 32178
904/328-1503

Santa Rosa County
501 Milton Street SW
Milton, FL 32570
904/623-2339

St. Johns County
P.O. Drawer O
St. Augustine, FL 32085
904/829-5681

Suwannee County
P.O. Drawer C
Live Oak, FL 32060
904/362-3071

Taylor County
P.O. Box 892
Perry, FL 32347
904/584-0888

Union County
P.O. Box 797
Lake Butler, FL 32054
904/496-3624

Volusia County
P.O. Box 2475
Daytona Beach, FL 32115
904/255-0981

Wakulla County
P.O. Box 598
Crawfordville, FL 32327
904/926-1848

Walton County
P.O. Box 29
DeFuniak Springs, FL 32433
904/892-3191

Washington County
P.O. Box 457
Chipley, FL 32428
904/638-4157

INDEX